**Praise**

Life Cou
SWEE



"Sinunu is like the best tour guide
our lives with simple and profound lessons from around the world. This book will not only charm you, but will remind you of the life you were meant to lead; sweet and full and peaceful."

—Bill O'Hanlon, author of *Do One Thing Different*

"It's not often that you come across a book that is entertainment, motivation, and travelogue all in one. With its concise anecdotes and multicultural charm, *Life Could Be Sweeter* is delightfully addictive and inspiring enough to have you rethinking your own priorities."

—Lynne Heitman, author of *First Class Killing*

"Bill takes us on an uplifting, real life journey of self and world exploration and helps us to experience the flavors of various cultures. We are encouraged to understand the richness of our differences and learn from others around the globe. Whether you have explored the world or just your own backyard, this is a must read for all!"

—Donna Sinnery,
vice president of Worldwide Staffing-
Financial Services

"Sinunu turns a wide-angle lens on the unique and wonderful ways our fellow travelers have sweetened life and offers simple suggestions and clear insights that can improve our lives. I couldn't wait to finish the book so I could start over again!"

—Glenn Sykes, managing director,
University of Chicago Graduate School
of Business Europe

# ABOUT THE AUTHOR

WILLIAM SINUNU, MA, LSW, is a licensed social worker who has counseled a wide variety of people, and was a flight attendant for almost twenty years before he was appointed the head of the Employee Assistance Program for JetBlue Airways in 2003. Sinunu has traveled to over 100 countries on six continents and lives in Forest Hills, NY.

# Life Could Be SWEETER

## 101 Great Ideas from Around the World for Living a More Rewarding Life

WILLIAM SINUNU

MARLOWE & COMPANY
NEW YORK

LIFE COULD BE SWEETER:
101 Great Ideas from Around the World for Living a More Rewarding Life



Published by
Marlowe & Company
An Imprint of Avalon Publishing Group Incorporated
245 West 17th Street • 11th floor
New York, NY 10011

AVALON
publishing group incorporated



Library of Congress Cataloging-in-Publication Data is available from the publisher.

ISBN 1-56924-374-3

9 8 7 6 5 4 3 2 1
*Book design by Maria E. Torres*

Printed in Canada

*In memory of Alex Sinunu—I miss you Dad.*

*This book is dedicated to the worldwide spirit of mutual respect. It is written to honor every individual who has positively impacted someone from another land. Most of all, it is dedicated to those who look for the best others have to offer—regardless of nationality or locale.*

*For my parents, Demi and Alex Sinunu, who presented travel as an exciting and manageable experience; for Era Kanes, who encouraged me to go for my dreams; for my global friends, who made each country an unpredictable adventure; for Tracy Hess, who radiates comfort and peace—thank you all.*

# CONTENTS

Introduction:
IN SEARCH OF CULTURAL INTELLIGENCE ❃ 1

Part 1
BASIC SIMPLICITY ❃ 9

Part 2
RECLAIMING TIME ❃ 37

Part 3
TEACH YOUR CHILDREN WELL ❃ 69

Part 4
TO YOUR HEALTH ❃ 109

Part 5
THIS THING CALLED LOVE ❃ 143

Part 6
EMBRACING YOUR SEXUALITY ❃ 167

Part 7
GOOD GRIEF ❃ 193

Part 8
EXPANDING YOUR COMFORT ZONE ❃ 219

Part 9
BE MY GUEST ❃ 259

Sources ❃ 305
Acknowledgments ❃ 311

# INTRODUCTION

## In Search of Cultural Intelligence

A JAPANESE FRIEND recently said to me: "America is *karoshi.*"

*Karoshi* is a Japanese word typically used to characterize an individual who lives at such a frantic pace that he or she becomes ill. But my friend was describing something much more ominous—a state of *karoshi* that has gripped our entire nation. Despite America's firmly entrenched sense of being "on top" of the world, we actually work more hours, enjoy less leisure time, suffer more depression and anxiety, have higher rates of obesity and heart disease, and endure more family violence than other nations—developed or developing—around the globe. But don't panic and don't despair. Although it may seem as though we're in a dire position—and make no mistake, if we continue on our current path, the outlook is grim—this book can help us get back on track!

Welcome aboard! You're invited to embark on an enlightening journey! You will be escorted on a fun and insightful front-seat, first-class uncharted tour of the traditions, values, and practices of other countries that can offer vital insights on how we might connect more deeply with those we love, take better care of our bodies and souls, and live more passionately in the present. There is, quite literally, a whole world of wisdom out there, one we're scarcely aware of, much less taking advantage of to enrich our own lives. My aim is to open up the possibility that there are other ways to live—ways that are already embraced by millions beyond our borders.

Let me be clear: This book is by no means "anti-American." Clearly, there is much to admire and enjoy about living in the U.S. I simply invite you to peek into other cultures, glimpse some of their healthiest practices and beliefs, then arrive at your own conclusions. Who knows? You may recognize aspects of other lifestyles that are beneficial to you and figure out ways to incorporate those lessons into your own life—if you choose to do so.

Although I have always had a passport embossed with the American eagle, I am a different kind of American. The son of a U.S. executive, I was born in Lebanon and shortly afterward moved with my family to Pakistan. From an early age, I experienced the striking absence of cross-cultural awareness among most Americans. In the midsixties, when I was six years old, the Pakistan-India War escalated and my family evacuated the area and temporarily returned to the United States. On my first day of elementary school, I was given a competency exam. The directions were to write the first letter of a word under its picture—an "m" under a picture of a mailbox, a "c" under a cat, and so on. I turned in a nearly blank sheet: my only response was an "r" under a picture of a bicycle. Immediately, my teachers concluded that I should be put back a grade. But I was not developmentally impaired; I simply had never seen a mailbox. They didn't exist in Pakistan. Nor were cats common pets, although I used to ride camels and elephants regularly after school. And, to me, the picture of a bicycle looked a lot like a rickshaw.

After a short stay outside Philadelphia, I didn't live in the United States again until I was eighteen. During that time away, I had the opportunity to live and travel in a number of countries. When my family settled in Athens, I came to appreciate the familial and personal rewards of a slower pace of life. In Cairo, I experienced the generosity and hospitality of people who had little. Absorbing the customs and values of many different cultures, I made some critical life decisions early on. I would never allow career and financial gain, and the frantic pace they dictate, to become the motivating focus of my life.

Nearly thirty years later, in September 1994, I was scheduled to be on a plane that crashed into the Pennsylvania countryside. At the last minute, on a whim, I changed plans and took an earlier flight. By grace and luck, I was alive. Or was I?

At the time, I lived in Chicago and was working seven days a week, juggling three commitments—work, full-time graduate school classes, and a social work residency with twenty patients. My life was a whirlwind. Like many Americans on a resolutely career-driven path, I had lost touch with my family and friends and lived in a chronic state of exhaustion. I had pledged to avoid getting caught up in the feverish pace our society calls "normal." How had this happened to me?

I scheduled a rushed, yet overdue, vacation to Puerto Rico to try to figure it out. On the flight to San Juan, I made a list of items I needed to buy once I got there—sun protection lotion, deodorant, and dental floss. Upon landing, I hopped in a cab for the short ride to my hotel in the Condado area. Upon unpacking, I hastily made my way to a local store. *Once I get everything I need, I can finally relax and think this through,* I told myself.

Walking into the small convenience store next door, I noticed the cashier having an animated conversation with a customer. The woman behind the counter was in her early fifties, with gray steaks through her coarse black hair and a wide, embracing smile. While she chatted with an older gentleman, I quickly found the items I was looking for and headed for the checkout area.

Standing in line behind three people, I shifted impatiently as the cashier smiled and greeted each customer. She made small talk with each person, asking about their families as she slowly rang up each item. I felt my lips tighten and my muscles contract. *Move it!* I fumed. Then it clicked. What was I thinking? Why was I upset with somebody who was simply being courteous, polite, and human? Furthermore, I was on vacation. What was my big rush?

I vowed to use my brush with death, along with my experience of a slower-paced culture, as opportunities to regain, and consciously maintain, the balance I had enjoyed prior to coming to this country. And it seems that I am not alone. There is growing evidence that Americans want more sanity and serenity in their lives. A survey of U.S. workers found that seventy percent experience an unhealthy balance between their work and personal lives. Furthermore, almost three times as many employees say family is their top priority as those who list work as their paramount concern. So why can't we make the leap to a more satisfying way of life?

Clearly, many of us long to jump off the endless treadmill of work, consumption, and still more work to pay for our ever-mounting collection of "stuff"—none of which brings us the sustenance we really need.

Meanwhile, most Americans are struggling to control their stress and dissatisfaction. In a recent ten-year period, the number of Americans being treated for depression more than tripled, while the number of those taking antidepressants doubled. Many of us cope with stress by overeating. Obesity has been declared a health epidemic and weight researchers estimate that if the current trend continues, in just twenty-five years every American will be overweight. Additionally, nearly a quarter of Americans suffer some kind of chronic, stress-related disease, from migraine headaches to back problems to gastrointestinal ailments. Seeking relief from these ailments, we are popping pills—from pain relievers to antianxiety medications—at record-breaking levels. But are we really addressing the root of the problems?

We try our best to support each other, but many of us struggle with relationship problems as well. Our divorce rate approaches sixty percent—the highest in the world. Meanwhile, our sex lives are typically less than enviable. The most recent data show that nearly one in five American marriages is sexless. And how are our kids faring? Each year more than 800,000 adolescents in the United States become pregnant, a rate nearly twice that of any other industrialized nation, while at least three million U.S. teens acquire a sexually transmitted disease. The latest cross-cultural study of teens around the globe shows American teens suffering substantially higher levels of depression than kids from other countries.

Clearly, our "normal" way of life—squeezed for time, dominated by work, infatuated with winning, disconnected from our loved ones—isn't working very well. How can we discover a "new normal"? I propose that we must develop a new mental and emotional muscle that I call "cultural intelligence." Using my own multicultural experiences as a launching pad, and drawing on the latest research and interviews with people across the globe, *Life Could Be Sweeter* explores how other countries and cultures approach a host of life issues, including work, time, parenting, consumption, health, relationships, sex, spirituality, loss, and community-building. Of course, not all cross-cultural practices are healthy or appropriate for Western readers—but many are surprisingly good fits. Here are some of the topics I consider on the pages that follow:

- Is stress really a necessary part of life? Maybe not. We'll look at how the Scandinavians minimize financial stressors, how the Jamaicans focus on the simple pleasures of life, and how the Hungarians maximize quality time.
- Do other cultures share our addiction to romance and finding the "perfect partner"—an ideal that so often crashes on the shoals of real-life marriage? I will present an array of intriguing approaches to love, including the Italian perspective on "over-the-top" romance, a Dutch couple who innovatively cohabitate without actually living together, and the European twenty-something singles with a way to figure out whether their current squeeze has long-term potential.
- Why are so many of us sexually obsessed—yet inhibited in the bedroom? I will show how the French juice up their sex lives with fantasy, how the Germans approach nudity, and how the Spanish comfortably inhabit their sexuality.
- Do we work to live or live to work? We'll take a look at dramatically different attitudes toward work in other countries, including some creative ways that citizens of Belgium, Ireland,

Holland, and the United Kingdom use their solid month per year (minimum!) of vacation time.

- According to the latest data, kids in the United States are more violent and rebellious than children in many other cultures. I will present an array of approaches to raising good kids, including the Cuban commitment to setting loving limits and the Finnish priority on building a "collaborative village." In addition, I will present international approaches to family bonding—from the Filipino norm of communal sleeping to the Ecuadorian *chalena*.
- How do people in many other cultures stay so slim? I will look at the French approach to walking, the Dutch approach to incorporating cycling into their daily lives, and the Indonesian approach to enjoying food without overeating.

This book is an invitation but also a bit of a dare, because we Americans are accustomed to seeing ourselves as the standard. Aren't other cultures supposed to look to *us* for how to live? Exploring the possibilities of other traditions requires a curious, open-minded willingness to confront the unknown. It is just this spirit of exhilarating adventure that *Life Could Be Sweeter* encourages and exemplifies. Catch the ride. I promise you the experience will be enjoyable and thought provoking—and just might change your life!

# 1
# Basic SIMPLICITY

# NORWEGIAN KNOW-HOW

EVEN THOUGH LARS and I had kept up over the years, I fidgeted nervously as the wheels hit the runway in Oslo. Sure, we had written and e-mailed each other, but we'd been school friends more than twenty years ago; would I even recognize him now? Would we still be compatible after all these years?

As the Customs doors swung open, Lars's tall, lanky frame stood out in the crowd and seemed to dwarf the doorway. There was no doubt it was him. The same head of tumbling blond curls, the same ear-to-ear, slightly crooked grin.

"Yo," I yelled out, followed by an exaggerated, "Ovah heah," my best attempt to sound like Sylvester Stallone. Lars had seen *Rocky* and told me I should sound like Stallone since I then lived in Philly. We both fell back laughing the way we used to do as kids; the kind of laugh that started deep in our guts and rushed like a vacuum through our chests and out through our mouths. Then we looked at each other and grinned.

"This is going to be a great week," I announced as we left the terminal and hopped into a cab.

As the taxi headed downtown, I watched the early morning

sun reflect off the snow. We sped past two cross-country skiers, both in ski suits and backpacks, nonchalantly poling down a path adjacent to the main road. I turned and stared at the pair behind us.

"Can't say I'd see *that* in Philly," I remarked.

"They're probably on their way to work," Lars casually responded.

"What a great way to commute," I said. "Good cardio exercise and no traffic worries."

Turning off the main road from the airport, we wound down narrow streets that seemed to slice the compact city into contrived, contemporary lanes. One of the central plazas was just coming alive as florists and coffee shops opened their doors. Even with my window down, I couldn't hear a peep, except for the icy breeze whistling through the cab. Although there were cars zipping about and people on the streets, I heard no horns honking or loud voices.

"The city is so quiet," I remarked.

"It's Norway," Lars responded. "Laid back and simple."

As Lars opened the front door to his apartment, I hesitated. As I peered into the front hall, the apartment looked strangely empty. Then I turned the corner and saw a simple, yet tasteful living area. A small beige couch sat between two small wooden end tables, each topped by functional chocolate-colored lamps. Across from the living room was a small dining area, complete with a simple pine table for six. The long, narrow apartment opened into a stand-up galley kitchen to one side and a bedroom to the other. There were none of the "extras" I was used to—pictures on the walls, knickknacks on display, or coasters on the table. Yet the room had a very inviting hip, retro feel.

"Your place is very cool," I said to Lars. "Clean lines."

"Really?" Lars surprisingly shrugged. "It's very typical Scandinavian. I don't know about cool. But if you say so!"

After I'd freshened up, Lars invited me to hang up my clothes in his closet. Opening the closet door, I saw three shirts, two pairs of slacks, and a pair of jeans.

"I'm a low-maintenance houseguest," I told him. "You didn't have to move your things to make room."

"I didn't," Lars said. I tried not to look shocked. Was that all the clothing he had?

"Come on, let's go meet Sonja," said Lars. "She lives right down the hall."

When we knocked, a tall, blue-eyed woman with a shy demeanor opened the door. She gave Lars a long, meaningful hug.

"I don't want to interrupt," I said with a smile. Sonja smiled and she extended her hand.

"So nice to meet you," she said taking my hand in both of hers. "Come in." Sonja's apartment was similar to Lars's space, except the living room had a plain blue couch perched in front of a wall of windows, whose sliding glass opened the way to a small balcony.

"Please sit, I have coffee on," Sonja said, returning a few moments later with three steaming mugs on a small tray. She plunked herself down on the floor.

"I like your minimalist style," I said looking around. "Very fresh and uncluttered."

Sonja shrugged. "*Lagom,*" she said.

"La what?" I asked, certain that I had misunderstood her. Sonja burst out laughing and rolled back on the floor.

"*Lagom.* Lars, help me. How do I explain *lagom* to Bill?"

Lars shook his head, "*Lagom* . . . it's hard to translate, but I think the best definition is 'enough.'"

"Yes," added Sonja with a nod. "Enough, nothing showy, we have just enough to be comfortable. It's the Scandinavian way."

That night I shifted and turned on the couch in Lars's living room, unable to sleep. Finally, I turned onto my side and slid my left hand under my pillow, propping my head up. Looking around the austere apartment, I thought about the many items I owned that I never used—from extra socks in the top dresser drawer to unopened toiletries in the bathroom to the electric can opener in the kitchen. I sighed and wondered, *"Do I* really *need all that stuff?"*

The next morning Lars and I rummaged around the galley kitchen for breakfast, playfully elbowing each other out of the way.

"I'll set the table," I said.

"Okay," Lars said, pointing to one of two cupboards. "Over there."

I opened the swinging wooden door to find exactly four dishes, four glasses, and four forks, knives, and spoons.

My mind was spinning. How often did I really use my own two sets of table settings for eight, one formal and one casual, along with linens, placemats, wine goblets, and water glasses? I sighed loudly.

"Are you okay Bill?" Lars asked placing his hand on my shoulder.

"It's nothing," I said managing a weak smile. Lars quickly called Sonja and she scooted down the hall, clad in robe and slippers, for breakfast. As the three of us sat at the wooden dining table and noshed on yogurt, sliced salmon, and pumpernickel bread, I talked about our American love for shopping and buying lots of "stuff."

"But so much of it I don't use," I lamented.

Sonja cocked her head to one side. "It's a simple solution. Don't buy it unless you have to!"

The next day, Sonja and I went for a long walk in the Vigeland Sculpture Park, passing the City Museum and the "Little Angry Boy" statue.

"I thought about what you said yesterday," Sonja reflected. "In Scandinavia, we live by the law of *jante.*"

"What is that?" I asked.

"It means we are low key about our assets and humble," she said quietly. "It just seems logical to me—live simply and don't waste."

"But don't you have any desire for luxurious things—maybe

a fancy car or nice jewelry?" I asked. I thought guiltily about my own Concord watch and Tumi luggage. Sonja rubbed her finger across her lips in thought.

"I don't think things bring happiness," she said. "In our country, to be flashy is considered gauche and disrespectful to others who have less."

Our original plan for a short walk turned into an invigorating three-hour jaunt through the leafless park and back into the downtown area, which was filled with small shops but retained an air of quiet and serenity. I could see my breath in the cold air.

"Not only is Oslo quiet, but I haven't seen a homeless person and I feel so safe," I noted.

"Can't you see?" Sonja said. "It's all tied into *jante.* We take care of those who have little. It is the main reason we have few homeless people and so little violence."

> Barry Schwartz, Swarthmore College professor and author of *The Paradox of Choice,* observes that despite a doubling of material possessions since 1950, the average American is significantly less happy today. The main culprit: Americans focus too much on things at the expense of relationships.

# JORDANIAN MIX-N-MATCH

I HEARD A voice faintly saying "Bill, Bill." Over the din of the crowd outside Customs at Amman International Airport, then I saw Rania's oval face bouncing above the sea of shoulders, disappearing and then reappearing as though she was jumping up and down on a pogo stick. I headed in her direction, weaving between people and poking my head up to make sure I was on track. Every couple of steps I would look up and catch Rania's eye as she continued to jump and wave. Finally I leaned in between two people, taking her hand.

"As always, you look amazing," I said, getting a good look at my old friend. Rania, a thirty-two-year-old Jordanian doctor whom I met in Chicago three years earlier, was stylishly outfitted in a black suit.

"You know the movie *Men in Black*? This is *Rania in Black*," she replied, twirling around, giggling. "But I'm glad you think it works!" she added, throwing her arms in the air and striking a model pose. We both laughed and, holding hands, barreled our way through the mob and out into the piercing Middle Eastern sun.

Although it was early in the morning, Rania's white subcompact car was already toasty. We drove along dusty roads and past several small stalls on the way to downtown Amman, passing several families walking alongside the highway. Most were clad in white robes and long white headdresses. Rania saw me staring at the pedestrians and understood my perplexed look. She said, "To protect them from the sun."

When we arrived at Rania's place, she gave me a tour of her tiny one-bedroom condo, daintily decorated in pastels with sheer curtains and frilly slipcovers.

"It's so bright and airy, Rania, great place," I said.

"Bright until you get to this," she grinned, pointing to her wardrobe of black items neatly arranged in a two-foot–wide closet.

Rania had selected one basic color—black—for her skirts, slacks, shoes, and purses. Her blouses often vary, but she always incorporates black, such as a black-and-white pin stripe or a black and red print.

"It's like 'mix and match' for professionals," she laughed, "but always solid black on the bottom half to keep my hips looking slim—well, slimmer."

The ledge at the top of the closet was piled with brightly accented scarves, gold brooches, shawls, and hats to create a number of different looks.

Rania observed, "I know black looks good on me so I stick with it, but I also like to add a little flair."

"How about the heat?" I winced.

"Dahling," she exaggeratedly cooed, "I'll put up with a little heat to look good!"

The next day as Rania and I strolled through Amman's main shopping area, I marveled at the endless parade of local shops with their merchandise displayed on the sidewalk, over the windows, and atop the doorframes.

"They don't miss a space here," I said.

"No," she responded, "but you certainly get an idea of everything they have just by walking by."

As we poked around the shops, I thought about Rania's stylish yet minimalist wardrobe.

"You seem like a smart consumer Rania," I said to her. "What's your secret?"

Running her hand along her chin, Rania said, "Well, I do have a few rules that I try to remember before every purchase. I ask myself, 'Do I really need this? Do I really love it? Is it made well?'" Deep in thought, Rania went on. "But my cardinal rule," she said, clapping her hands gently together in front of her face, "is to always go for quality. I buy the cheapest of the best, never the best of the cheapest. That way, I spend relatively little on clothes, but still have a good-looking wardrobe."

Later that week, Rania and I made a side trip to the tranquil beach resort city of Aqaba and swam in the salty Dead Sea. We laughed as we tried to snorkel and dive underwater, while the salt buoyed us quickly back to the surface. Rania then took me to the ancient city of Petra where we rode camels through the archaeological ruins and explored a two-floor, pink and orange stone monastery framed by classic sculpted columns.

The trip was exhilarating. However, back at home, I found myself thinking about Rania's sensible approach to looking terrific. Gazing inside my closet at the array of mismatched colors, I pulled out a pair of light green pants. "Strange color, must have been on sale," I muttered as I threw them on the bed. Then I pulled out a baby blue sweater with a badly stretched neck. "Poorly made," I sighed. By the time I'd plowed through my closet, more than half of my wardrobe lay on the bed. "One season wonder," "faded," "trendy," and "what was I thinking?" I murmured as I looked over various items. I didn't even know I had many of these clothes. I put the rejects in a bag and gave them to charity. It felt great to start with a clean slate!

Now, each time I shop, I mentally run through Rania's checklist. Blue, black, and khaki for shirts and slacks, along with black for shoes and belts. Keeping things simple and focused, I built a limited, functional, and tasteful matching wardrobe. I now wear what I buy and I have extra cash for things I enjoy—like traveling!

According to psychologist Thomas Spencer, Americans wear approximately twenty percent of the clothes they own.

# FESTIVE FRIENDS

MARRIED FOR TWENTY-TWO years, my friends Eduoard and Martine live just outside Paris in a comfortable two-bedroom condo with their teenage son. Martine is a warm, bubbly woman in her midforties, birdlike, with a pert nose and red hair cut in a bob and tucked behind her ears. Eduoard, in his early fifties, has a lean runner's physique and gray hair around the temples that sets off his bald pate and round, open face.

They host an annual *"grand dîner"* for twenty friends. "Join us so we can spoil you and thank you for your friendship," cajoled Martine in her transatlantic phone invitation.

"I would be delighted," I responded.

The magical evening, set for mid-September, started at four PM. I rang the doorbell of their apartment on the Left Bank at four-thirty and upon entering their apartment, noticed that there was one other guest in the room. *"Damn,"* I thought. I had forgotten the French were typically "fashionably late." On the other hand, arriving "early" gave me the chance to see my friends' transformed apartment.

And what a transformation! As I looked around the flower-filled room, a white-gloved waiter in an elegant tuxedo approached me with a tray of champagne and a broad smile.

"Roberrrt!" I cried, taking the tray out of his hand and placing it on a side table. I embraced Martine and Eduoard's son with a hug. Then I playfully pushed him away, stepped back, and surveyed him from head to toe.

"You really cleaned up!" I remarked.

He blushed, picked up the tray, and with a playfully professional accent, asked *"Le champagne?"*

*"Mais oui,"* I responded with an equally exaggerated formality. *"Merci bien."*

Sipping my Moet, I scanned the apartment. An opulent arrangement of white lilies and red roses fanned out atop a draped, pearl-beaded tablecloth on the dining-room table. The sun, just starting to set in the late September sky, lit up the veranda and reflected into the apartment, creating hues of warm orange and sun-kissed yellow. Turning, I accidentally nudged a tall, statuesque blond woman in her fifties, wearing a low-cut black dress with eyes made-up dramatically, eyelids accentuated by blue arches. She stepped back and held her champagne glass up to steady its contents.

*"Ah, je m'excuse,"* I said.

She smiled. *"Pas problème,"* she casually reassured me. *"Je m'appele Bernadette,"* she introduced herself, holding out her hand.

*"Mon nom est* Bill," I said, taking her hand and kissing her once on each cheek. Our white-gloved waiter brought a huge circular cheese platter and placed it on the center of the table directly in front of the flowers.

*"Ah, le fromage,"* Bernadette exclaimed looking at the arrangement. *"C'est magnifique!"* The cheeses, arranged like a clock with a different cheese at each hour, were intentionally placed to represent increasing intensity of flavors as time progressed.

Bernadette and I decided to sample each cheese, starting with a very mild Gouda at twelve and making our way around the clock. As guests arrived, Martine met each of them at the door with outstretched arms and a kiss on each cheek, parading them around the room and introducing them to the other equally sociable friends. Scrumptious canapés, including linen-lined trays of pâtés and fresh crab, arrived over the next several hours as the last glint of sunset nestled into candlelit darkness. By the time we sampled the sharp Stilton at eleven o'clock, all the guests had met and the apartment was filled with the energy and laughter of a synergistic gala.

Our magical evening progressed with a leisurely stroll to a neighborhood restaurant. I gasped when I walked into the dimly lit private room, which was decorated with shooting arrangements of red roses in each corner. An enormous round candlelit table, draped in white linens and set with rows of gleaming silver utensils, dwarfed the room. Four waiters standing just inside the door wearing crisp white jackets and creased napkins on their arms escorted guests to their seats.

Once the guests were seated, Martine raised her champagne and looked around the table with a smile. The room came to a gradual hush as one by one the guests silently held up their glasses.

"To our friends," Martine whispered as a single tear trickled down her cheek. "To the family we have the luxury of choosing. Each of you is very special to us. Thank you for joining us tonight."

Bernadette, with yet another glass of Moet in hand, leaped up and breathlessly described how she had met Martine and Eduoard.

"I saw him first and thought *'très beau,'*" she said coquettishly, holding up her napkin to cover her face up to her eyes and exaggeratingly batting her eyelashes. Eduoard's full cheeks flushed red as the group roared. Martine, rocking and clapping, shrieked with laughter.

Then Jasmine, a neighbor of Martine and Eduoard, coyly stood, "Our balcony has a slightly better view of the Tour d'Eiffel *and* the Arc de Triomphe than our hosts." Eduoard shook his head and wagged his finger at her. *"Pas vrai!"* The guests chuckled.

"So one evening my sister and I," Jasmine motioned to Jeanette, "invited Martine and Eduoard for a second cup of coffee and croissants on our terrace to prove it." Walking toward her hosts, Jasmine took Martine's and Eduoard's hands in her own. She leaned down and gave them each a kiss on the cheek. "That was twenty-five years ago. With friends like you, it seems like just yesterday," Jasmine said with a tremulous smile. As her sister Jeanette started to clap and blow kisses across the table, the rest of the group joined in the applause.

The next afternoon I made arrangements to meet Martine and Eduoard at a café. "That was a magnificient evening," I told them. "There was so much love, fun, and gratitude." Sitting between them, I reached out and hugged them both, one arm around each of my friends.

As Eduoard grew misty-eyed, Martine reached out and took his hands. "Life is about cherishing and appreciating the people in our lives," she said quietly.

I nodded. "Well, I just want to let you know how honored I am to be included," I told them.

"We love you," Martine said, taking my face in her hands and kissing my cheek.

"Besides," Eduoard chuckled, throwing his hands up, "What else would we spend our money on?"

Martine smiled impishly. "Maybe a dishwasher," she asked with raised eyebrows.

"Ha!" responded Eduoard. "I don't recall anyone on their deathbed looking up at their spouse and saying 'remember that time we went shopping? I'm so glad we bought that dishwasher!'"

"But last night?" Eduoard said, his face lighting up. "That is a night to remember!"

According to psychologist Paul Rozin of the University of Pennsylvania, Europeans spend a greater percentage of their disposable income on *experiences* such as vacation packages and concert tickets, while Americans spend more of their money on *goods* such as cars and air-conditioners.

# HIDDEN RICHES

MY FRIEND TRACY and I had five days off. Looking out the window at the blowing snow hammering Philadelphia in mid-February, we said "Beach time!"

"We are looking for sun—any place warm," I told the agent at the airport. She scanned her computer.

"How about Cancun—there are still a few seats in first class."

I looked at Tracy *"Ya, ya, ya, arriba!"* I hooted. "And first class to boot!"

"Let's do it," Tracy smiled. Within twenty minutes, we were airborne to Mexico, sipping champagne in seats 2A and 2C.

"Give it to me!" demanded the young girl, grabbing her brother's computer game.

"Mom," the boy wailed, "Trisha took my Gameboy!"

As a scuffle ensued, Tracy looked at me with raised eyebrows. "Could be a long flight," I muttered. She held up her finger and smiled. Stretching forward, she rummaged through the seat pocket and pulled out two headsets. But for the next few hours, the loud-pitched shrieks from the row behind us pierced even our headsets, making the flight a nerve-wracking ordeal.

Six hours later, lying on the beach in sun-drenched Cancun, we'd forgotten all about airborne sibling rivalry. As I settled onto my lounge chair, I noticed a local family of ten, playing tag on the beach. They were laughing and running in the shallow waters. Each older child held a younger one by the forearms as they chased each other through the surf. Meanwhile, the parents lay face up on a small, tattered blanket with the husband resting his head on his wife's belly. The father cheered his kids on while the mother smiled at the entire clan. When the kids came back to the blanket for lunch, everybody pitched in, offering food to the others before serving themselves. After the meal, the family cleaned up and went for a walk along the beach, all holding hands, with the youngest seated on her father's shoulders beaming. As the sun set, the entire group squealed with laughter as they crammed into their small, dented car and drove off toward home. I turned to Tracy, who had also been watching the family.

"Nice," she murmured.

"The way it should be," I added.

> The best things in life are free.

# LIMA FAMILY LOVE

A FEW YEARS ago, in Lima for a day en route to Cuzco and Machu Picchu, I'd hired a guide to show me the city. Maria was a soft-spoken, slightly heavy-set woman in her late forties, with streaks of gray running through her shoulder-length hair. As Maria drove me through the ancient city, she pointed out various points of historical interest.

After a half hour of gazing at churches and monuments, I turned to her and said, "Forget the tourist sights."

Maria looked at me, perplexed.

"I want to experience how real Peruvians live," I said. Silently, Maria drove on for another minute, and then turned the wheel sharply to the right. As we started to climb a steep hill, she smiled at me, revealing a shiny silver tooth behind her full lips.

"Okay," she said with a smile. "Let's go."

As we drove over the hill, the roads turned from gravel into dirt and there were fewer and fewer signs of people. Finally, Maria pulled the car to the side of the road in front of a thick row of trees. "Come meet my family," she said simply. I followed Maria into the woods, ducking to avoid the thick brush and paddling with my hands to push aside the flailing branches. After plowing past some twenty trees, we came upon a small clay structure. Four small children, all shoeless and dressed in tattered clothes, came running toward Maria, singing her name and jumping about her feet. Laughing, Maria knelt down for a group hug. She introduced me as "*Señor* Bill" and the oldest child, Manuel, a boy of about seven, smiled shyly and said "*Hola, Señor* Bill." He then went running into the woods with the other three squealing after him.

Maria brought me into their home, one large room with a dirt floor and no furniture, only a few blankets. There were a couple of carved-out ledges that served as windows, without glass and covered with uneven material serving as curtains. I stared at one ledge with two skulls propped up on it. Maria's eyes teared up. "My grandparents," she said softly. "They keep watch over us." I shivered and put my hand on her shoulder.

When Maria invited me for lunch, I accepted but I felt a pang of guilt and wondered if they could afford to have a guest. Maria, her four children, her mother, and I sat cross-legged on a blanket in front of tortillas and beans. As we held hands in a circle, Manuel said a prayer before eating. Maria carefully gave each child her attention, dribbling the beans over each tortilla, forming the first letter in each child's name. The children squealed with delight and the youngest jumped up clapping, "Pedro, Pedro!"

The kids were excited to have a guest and unfailingly polite, saying "*gracias*" whenever they were offered something. Shortly after lunch, Maria drove me back to my hotel.

"We don't have a lot of money, but we are happy," Maria said.

"No Maria," I finally said as we approached downtown. "You may have few *things*, but you are very *rich*."

> Betsy Taylor, founder and president of the Center for a New American Dream, a nonprofit group that helps Americans resist excessive commercialism, and author of *What Kids Really Want That Money Can't Buy*, asserts that despite children's pleas for material goods, what they actually desire are time, love, and attention.

# TURKMEN HOSPITALITY

MY COUSIN MICHELE, a tall, attractive twenty-two-year-old with a slender face and long jet black hair, decided to join the Peace Corps. When I answered my portable phone, I heard her voice gleefully blurt out, "I got it! I got my assignment: Turkmenistan."

After a lull, I responded, "Wow, that's great!" As she filled in the details, I meandered through my apartment in search of an atlas. I found the country between Afghanistan and Russia.

Once Michele landed in the capital city of Ashgabat, her senses were on fire. Her ears were assaulted by a strange, distinctly guttural and seemingly harsh language. She felt suddenly very alone, knowing that very few people spoke English. Would she ever master Turkmen, the local language? She also found herself staring at the fashions—the men were clad in Western slacks and collared shirts, but the women wore long, brilliantly hued cotton dresses and head scarves. *"At least they get to wear lots of bright colors,"* Michele thought to herself, knowing she would probably start dressing like a local.

As she settled into the seat of the ancient train with dirty windows for the slow, screeching ride to the village just north of the Afghanistan border, Michele felt her heart and mind race. *"I wonder what my host family will be like. What will the living conditions be like? I am supposed to teach health topics to the locals—will they be receptive?"* Michele silently bumped along on the hot, dusty twelve-hour train ride, at times shoulder-to-shoulder with locals, at other times virtually alone. Watching the passing countryside through streaked windows, Michele caught glimpses of endless brown, cracked tundra, and shivered.

From the remote train station, a Peace Corps-sponsored driver picked up Michele to take her on the short ride to her host family's home. The car stopped short in front of a small structure, engulfing it in a cloud of dust. Through itchy eyes, Michele could see a modest house along with a small shack alongside it. *"Neighbors, I guess,"* she thought to herself. The driver turned and nodded at Michele with a toothless smile. Wiping the sweat and dust from her face, Michele picked up her suitcase, thanked him and waved good-bye.

Standing beside the house next to a cow, with chickens swarming around her feet, was a slim, sturdy woman. When she caught sight of Michele, her wrinkled, brown face broke into a smile. Dropping the bucket she was holding, she walked a few steps toward Michele, and then, holding her dress a couple of inches above the ground with one hand, she broke into a sprint, plastering her flailing scarf to her head with her other hand. The woman wrapped Michele in a bear hug and spun her around.

"I didn't understand a word she said as she smiled and chatted through her gold teeth," Michele reminisced tearily. "But I instantly felt her warmth. The twinkle in her eyes told me about her kindness *and* her strength."

One of the greatest compliments in Turkmen society is to be a *"myhmansoyer"* or "lover of guests." Michele's host family—mother Bibi who collected a small government pension, her twenty-seven-year-old son Serdar a geography teacher, Serdar's wife, Aygul, who held an esteemed government job, and their two toddlers—exemplified this quality. Because she was the honored guest, Michele was given her own room. Everyone else shared common space. Although there was no furniture, there were plenty of cushions and the pride of Turkmenistan—beautiful oriental rugs.

"When I first arrived, I didn't know what to do, where to sit or how to act. So I just smiled a lot, watched, and followed their lead."

Bibi showed Michele around and Michele learned that the small shack next door was actually an outhouse with a primitive toilet and a shower area that consisted of a cold water spigot, a bucket, and a hole in the floor.

"I had to adjust to the living conditions," she admitted. "But it didn't take me long."

In her two-year stay, Michele learned much about the

Turkmen way of life. Bibi budgeted the family income carefully, always managing to save a small amount for emergencies, however never at the expense of making people feel welcome and comfortable. Guests were fawned over and spoiled with food, drink, and attention.

Michele's experience was cut short by the events of September eleventh and Turkmenistan's close proximity to Afghanistan. With one day's notice, the Peace Corps ordered Michele home. When Bibi heard the news, she left the house in tears and was gone for several hours. As Michele threw her few belongings into her suitcase, Bibi entered Michele's room and gave her two gifts.

"For your family," Bibi said, presenting her with a plastic treasure chest and two small tea cups. Michele started to sob uncontrollably. She held Bibi close and felt her host mother's tears on her shoulder.

"Here was a gift," Michele told me later in a halting voice, "that would cost a couple of dollars for us, but amounts to a month's pay for Bibi and her family. It is the most meaningful present I have ever received."

According to a study examining the effect of close relationships on health and well-being by University of Michigan psychologist Stephanie Brown, it's better to give than receive! The study found that older adults who do not help others are more than twice as likely to pass away as those who do help out.

# 2
# Reclaiming TIME

# JAMAICAN JAM

I HAD WORKED two sixty-hour weeks straight and badly needed a break. By the time I arrived at Montego Bay airport, my shoulders felt as though they were knotted around my ears. Even by the third morning in the quiet, tropical beach town of Negril, I still couldn't relax. Rubbing my aching temples, I realized that my mind was racing with things I had to do when I got home. "*Why can't I just let go?*" I wondered.

That afternoon, I wandered down to the beach in Negril, an endless stretch of silky white sand that wrapped around spread out below lush, unspoiled foliage. At the end of an isolated strip of beach was a small shack framed by an arching palm tree, with a few tables and chairs, right at the water's edge. *A perfect spot for a light lunch,* I thought, poking my head into the shack to announce my presence. There I saw a large, middle-aged Jamaican woman standing behind a counter. When she saw me, a huge dazzling smile lit up her round face.

"Come on in my friend," she invited me. "My name is Daphne. And you—you look troubled. Try one of these!" She pointed to a blender surrounded by ripe island fruits. "You have to juice, baby. Bananas, kiwi, melon, throw them all in together and you'll live forever." She threw her head back, revealing three ample chins and exclaimed, "Yes, baby, life is to enjoy! Every day, enjoy every moment!"

I managed a smile as Daphne ambled toward me, gathering up three other tourists standing in line and raising the volume on her tape player.

"It's conga time, Jamaican–style, baby. Time for you people to loosen up!" The German threesome and I looked at each other, shrugged, and smiled as Daphne threw her hands in the air and led us into the surf, swaying and singing,

"Oh no *mon,* no sad faces here in Jamaica." The five of us danced together in the turquoise ripples of the water, all the while sipping Daphne's magic fruit elixir and laughing until our stomachs hurt. Daphne whooped and hollered, holding the hem of her floral skirt a few inches above her ankles with one hand and waving with the other. Shaking her ample bosom and behind to the beat, she splashed and hooted. "Yes baby, this is life." Suddenly, one of the German men suddenly stopped and glanced at his watch.

"Oh no, not at Miss Daphne's party," our hostess scolded, shaking her finger playfully at her newfound friend. "All the watches come off, baby." Reaching toward him, she unsnapped his watch and slipped it into his pocket, then grabbed his hands and began to dance. "Life is to enjoy," she reminded him. "Just laugh and let it all go. Make life a vacation."

The sun was sinking into the Atlantic, but I was still having too much fun to leave. The Germans went back to their hotel, but Daphne and I danced on. I didn't know what time it was and I didn't care. Finally, I hugged Daphne and thanked her for a wonderful afternoon.

"You have a beautiful soul," she told me. "Let it live."

I felt tears well up. She winked at me as I turned and walked toward my rental car, feeling calmer and happier than I had in months. That night, I slept like a baby.

> New research by psychologist Martin Seligman shows that the happiest, healthiest people make time for activities that get them into "flow"—that delicious experience of total absorption in the present moment.

# INDIAN INNER PEACE

IT WAS THE first time I'd gone on vacation by myself and I was apprehensive. I had a block of time off that didn't coincide with those of my travel buddies and I'd been meaning to return to London. I decided to just go for it and discover how traveling alone panned out. As I walked in front of Buckingham Palace, I found myself feeling a bit nostalgic and wanting to share my excitement with my friends. The second night there, as I "queued up" in Leicester Square awaiting the release of that night's half-price theater tickets, I met Rose, a chocolate-toned beauty with long black hair. Surrounded by the neon lights and advertisements of this bustling part of the city, we started chatting. We watched an older man with a long, tattered black coat break into a political rant criticizing the prime minister. Then a teenage girl with spiky black hair and large black boots broke into song as her young companion passed his hat down our line and said "cheers" as the coins clinked together.

"This may be actually more entertaining than the theater," Rose laughed.

Born and raised in Bombay, Rose told me about her early,

colorful life growing up in India and how she had adapted to her new life in England, working as an architect. I couldn't help noticing that whenever she smiled, her face radiated serenity. After buying our tickets, we decided to continue our conversation over lunch. We laughed and talked as we strolled, weaving through cobblestoned lanes alongside quaint pubs and cafes.

"You have such a calm way about you," I marveled as we savored tandoori at a local Indian restaurant in Covent Garden. "I'm jealous! What's your secret?"

Rose leaned toward me. "Close your eyes," she whispered, "and adjust your posture so you are upright but not rigid."

"Huh," I responded, thoroughly confused.

"Just try it," she gently urged.

Obediently, I closed my eyes and followed Rose's rhythmic slowly-spoken directions.

"Now rest your hands on your knees, palms upright," she quietly directed me. "Focus on your breathing and let your mind become as empty as possible."

Easier said than done, I thought a bit grumpily, as my mind almost immediately began to bubble with memories and plans.

"If you wander into thinking, return gently to the practice of mindlessness," Rose instructed, as though she had read my thoughts. "Let yourself move into the new realm." It was hard to stay focused on nothing, but on the third try it took.

Gradually, I felt my heart rate slow as my entire body calmed down and relaxed. My shoulders eased while my neck seemed to actually lengthen. When Rose and I said our good-byes, I noticed that my anxiety level had plunged and my concerns about traveling alone had disappeared. I greeted passers-by on the streets with a smile that was readily returned. The next day I rented a car and drove to Brighton where the beach seemed more alive than I had remembered and the crisp breeze particularly invigorating. For over an hour, I sat on the sand and watched a gull aimlessly circle a lighthouse, wondering what life would be like as a seagull. *"Wouldn't that be nice?"* I smiled to myself. *"No clocks, no schedules, no deadlines, no stress!"*

I now make the time every day to meditate. After just a few minutes of quiet focus, I feel rested and rejuvenated, as though I'd just taken a peaceful nap. Thank you, Rose!

Dr. David Orme-Johnson, the dean of research at Maharishi International University in India, reports that as the frequency of meditation increases, stress levels decrease.

# BRAZILIAN BREATHS

JAN, A FRIEND in her early fifties who lost her husband two years ago after a lengthy illness, called me. "Come over please. I need your help," she said. I arrived at her house in twenty minutes. Jan took my hands in hers.

"I know you won't judge me," she said, her shoulders relaxing and her face breaking into a smile. "I am going to get work done in Brazil," she said as she pushed her cheeks upward, lifting her face. "It is less than half the price here. Would you be willing to come and be with me through the recuperation?" she asked.

"As long as you are comfortable with your decision, I am here for you," I said.

Jan and I went to Rio a few days before her surgery to get settled. We strolled along Copacabana Beach, amazed at the number of physically fit and attractive people. Looking up at the huge statue of Christ that overlooks the city, Jan, known for her self-deprecating sense of humor, threw her arms straight up, tilted her chin skyward, and blurted out "Oh God, can you help me look like her!" nodding at a statuesque, glowing young woman with jet black hair. We both broke into hysterics!

Jan sailed through surgery with no complications. Still mindful of my need to be responsible and check back on Jan, I contemplated my options for the day. I made my way to the hotel gym while Jan napped. Hoping for a yoga or Pilates class, I scanned the board. There was only a "Deep Breathing" class starting shortly. I walked into the class studio to find lines of people lying side by side on blue mats, as relaxed as kindergartners at nap time.

For the next thirty minutes, I breathed in long, exhilarating breaths that plumped and pumped my body with oxygen. It was a marked contrast to my regular breathing routine of short, shallow gasps. I was stunned at how calm I began to feel. Tightening up my stomach muscles and letting them loosen as I inhaled, I learned to fill my lungs and eventually my belly with air through my nose. Then I would force all the air out of my body through my mouth, making a series of noises while getting the last breaths buried deep within me out.

"Replenish your body with clean air," the instructor said. "Get all the old stale air out."

After the class, I felt energized and more alert than I had in weeks. *"A perfect prelude to tackle and tour the city in the upcoming days,"* I thought to myself. After a relaxing walk on the beach and several deep breaths of fresh salt air, I returned to the hotel where I slept better than I had in months.

I now practice this ritual at work during the day. I take a few minutes to breathe and get the stale air out. It is a wonderful rejuvenator!

> According to Dr. Shachi Shantinath, senior researcher in the Psychology Department at the University of Fribourg in Switzerland, proper deep breathing is imperative for physical and psychological well-being.

# ARAB ANSWERS

MAHMOUD, A CHECK-IN clerk for a small bed-and-breakfast in Casablanca, has a broad smile that lights up his cocoa skin. When I traveled through North Africa with two friends, he warmly welcomed us to the B & B and helped us plan our itinerary.

"You must go to Marrakech if you want to see the real Morocco," he insisted. "I can take you there if you like."

We left modern Casablanca for the short train ride to traditional Marrakech. Entering the old city, we walked into the dusty open-air market (the *"souk"* in Arabic), crammed with rows of ornate rugs, beautiful pieces of woodwork, and fine leathers for sale. Our appetites were tantalized by the mouth-watering aromas of spices that permeated the city from the open grills.

Sitting in a café, we were entranced by all of the activity—an expert juggler nearby throwing bananas into the air and a storyteller to the side surrounded by a swarm of mesmerized children. I gasped as a snake charmer seated directly in front of us played his sinuous tune as a long, gray snake coiled up in the air. As magicians and acrobats joined the group in the main square, I felt as though I had front row seats for the Arabian Circus. I found myself wondering, too, how Mahmoud could make time to show three strangers the delights of his country.

Mahmoud then led us to a quiet restaurant for a delicious local lunch. As we squatted on brightly colored pillows around a beautiful inlaid table, a server moved around the table, pouring perfumed water from a silver urn over our right hands. Mahmoud then clapped his hands and we were served a sumptuous meal of chicken tajine (a spicy stew that had simmered for hours), couscous, and mint tea. The scents of coriander, cumin, saffron, and marjoram made my nostrils tingle. Mahmoud beamed from ear to ear: he seemed to enjoy himself as much as we were.

"How come you are always so happy?" I asked Mahmoud.

"My life is one quarter work, one quarter family, one quarter friends, and one quarter *me*," he said.

I was intrigued. "What does the one quarter 'you' mean?" I asked.

He smiled. "I am responsible for my own happiness. So I take the time to make me number one."

Mahmoud explained that he takes one day a week to shut the world out and focus on his own life. He doesn't answer the phone and he spends the day in complete silence.

"What do you *do*?" I asked, unable to imagine tolerating such self-imposed isolation.

"I ask myself questions," he responded. "Am I happy? Am I the person I want to be? Usually the answer is yes, so I then wonder what can I do to bring even greater life satisfaction—some new hobby I may want to try, somebody I want to meet, or someplace I want to go. I write it all down."

I still had a couple days off after my trip, so I tried it when I got home. Countless distractions beckoned and I felt uneasy starting a new routine. *"I'll just check my e-mail,"* I thought to myself. Although I turned off the phone, I still found myself thinking, *"I bet I have messages."* Finally, I sat on the couch and said to myself, defiantly, "Now what?" But by mid-morning, the day started to take on a new feel. I stretched out on the couch and wrapped myself up in my favorite blanket. As thoughts came into my head, I jotted them down on a pad of paper, which I placed on the coffee table next to the couch. That afternoon I looked over my scribble: "Call my brothers, reconnect with Jorge, Vernon, Giovanna, and Maria (friends I hadn't talked to in some time), and check out the new yoga center in town." Feeling relaxed and peaceful, I drifted off for a deep two-hour nap. I awoke feeling rejuvenated, though I'd been on a weekend vacation. Initially, a day centered solely on me felt selfish and self-indulgent, I began to realize that the more centered I am, the more I can actually give to others.

Now, once a month, I wake up and scamper around my apartment in anticipation of my "reflect and recharge" day. I turn off the phone and answering machine and I never turn on the computer or television. I don't look at the mail and I don't answer the door. In fact, I don't even shower or dress! It's simply a day of complete silence that allows me some time to connect with my thoughts, feelings, and priorities.

> An Australian study on health, supported by The University of Newcastle and the University of Queensland, shows that leisure time contributes to health and well-being and may decrease moderate levels of stress.

# NORWEGIAN MARATHONS

RUTH, A FRIEND from college, told me about her experience in Norway. After graduation, Ruth worked for a multinational U.S. company. As for most Americans in managerial roles, long work weeks and endless project lists became the norm. Two years into her role, exhausted and desperate for a change, Ruth jumped at the chance for a temporary assignment in the Oslo office.

Ruth immediately noticed that she was the only one putting in her standard twelve-hour days. But she also realized that although the others in the office arrived late and left early, they were very focused on work while in the office. Walking across the office for a third cup of coffee late one morning, she asked one of her peers, Sven, who had just arrived, about the office work habits.

He smiled. "Although we are an American company, we are Norwegians and that means no face time," he said with twinkling eyes. "Work is work. We get in here, get it done, and get on to other parts of our lives."

According to Anders Hayden, author of *Sharing the Work, Sharing the Planet,* although the Norwegian workweek is about thirty-seven hours, hourly productivity of Norwegian workers was ten percent higher than American workers in 2001.

# GERMAN GALLIVANTING

TRACY, DIRK, AND I were having a blast in Chile. Stretching down the entire West coast of South America, this long, slender country offers a number of delights. My friends and I spent two days in bustling, cosmopolitan Santiago, where we toured some of the local attractions, including poet Pablo Neruda's home. Then we hopped a flight north to the dusty Attacama Desert, then went hiking and biking through the sand trails and exploring some of the oasislike natural springs. Then we flew to the mountainous resort town of Pucon for some whitewater rafting.

Five of us were assigned to a raft—the three of us plus Uta and Werner, an attractive, outgoing young couple.

"Are you German?" Dirk asked.

"*Ja,*" Uta answered, "Ve are Chermans from Cologne." We all chuckled as they playfully exaggerated their accents. Werner explained that they were accountants and in the midst of a four-month journey around the world.

After an invigorating, roller coaster–like ride down the river, amid swirling tides and shrieks of laughter, the five of us lay exhausted on the shore.

"How do you just take off on a four-month trip?" I asked. "I want to sign up for that!" Uta ran her fingers through Werner's hair as they smiled at each other.

"We saved our money for a year and negotiated additional leaves with our companies," she said. "Long vacations are common in Europe, so four months isn't as radical as it sounds."

Added Werner, "Plus, traveling to countries where we know nobody and speak just a few words in other languages is an adventure—and in my opinion, the best education."

"But how will this affect your career paths?" Dirk asked, his voice tinged with anxiety. Uta smiled at Dirk.

"It's only four months," she reminded him gently. "Put your working life on a timeline and you'll see it's a small amount of time. We have our whole lives to work."

Werner leaned back and propped up his head with his wrist. "Uta and I are both twenty-eight," he said thoughtfully. "We will blink and be thirty-five. Blink again and we will be fifty-five. Life is short and will go even faster as we get older. We want no regrets."

"That's how I want to live," I said softly.

"Then you have a European attitude toward life," grinned Werner. "We work to live, not live to work."

That night, we relaxed at the lodge in front of a roaring fire and sipped Chilean wine. Tracy made a toast, "To Uta and Werner, who *live* life."

Dirk raised his glass, adding, "Hear, hear, and to meeting people from other lands who have so much to teach us."

I sat quietly thinking about my own life. *"Forget about the raise next year,"* I thought to myself. *"I can always live on less money. I am going for some time off."*

According to Paul Swaim, an economist with the Organization for Economic Cooperation and Development, Europeans work about one-third less than Americans. In fact, most Europeans work well under forty hours per week and have up to two months of vacation per year. Additionally, employees are guaranteed to start at a minimum of twenty days off per year. In Australia, Belgium, Ireland, Holland, Switzerland, and the United Kingdom, many long-term employees amass vacation blocks of several months per year.

# VIEWS FROM THE PEAK

PETER IS A forty-two-year-old flight attendant, based in Chicago with seventeen years of seniority. For fifteen years, he traveled constantly, either for his job or on vacations. "Then I hit a rut and decided I wanted to do something different with my life," he recalled. Peter returned to school and received his MBA from prestigious Northwestern University. But then what? Peter was at a crossroads.

"I had the high-powered degree and a number of corporate suitors, but there was something that was holding me back from leaving my flying job and segueing into a new profession," he said. "I just couldn't do it."

Peter put everything on hold and took off for the hilltops of Peru to think it through. Maria, a Peruvian hiker who was leading Peter's four-day hike along the Incan Trail and up the mountain peaks, plunked herself down next to Peter during a snack break. Peter, who looked withdrawn and sullen, gazed out at the rolling green hills.

"Would you like to talk about it?" Maria asked.

Without responding, Peter wrapped his arms tightly around his knees. Maria touched Peter's forearm and said, "Sometimes it helps to talk it through with a good listener."

Suddenly, his eyes filled. "I have to make a decision," he whispered, "and I don't know what to do."

After a moment of shared silence, Maria pulled out a pen and a piece of paper from her backpack and drew a line down the middle. Gently she touched the side of his arm and placed the paper and pen beside him.

"List the pros of change on one side and the cons on the other," she suggested. "It might help you gather your thoughts and see your choices more clearly." Maria stood up and rejoined the other hikers who were sharing a snack a few feet away.

Peter recalled: "There I was sitting atop Machu Picchu, the site of an ancient Incan civilization, with puffy clouds nipping at my scalp, looking down at the rolling hills of endless green, trying to put my life thousands of miles away in perspective."

At that moment, Peter realized that while he felt he "should" change his career and do something to make more money, he didn't really want to. *"Our American priorities are usually power, prestige, and wealth,"* he mused. *"That isn't true for me. I value free time and am just not an office person."* He shared his revelations with Maria.

"Do the job you love and follow your passion," she responded, smiling. "You'll get much older faster if you're not happy."

"You are so wise," Peter told her.

"Well," Maria acknowledged, "I was a psychologist for ten years before I realized my real love is nature. So here I am. And—coincidentally or maybe not so coincidentally—here *you* are."

Peter had already found his niche—he just had to step out of his element to think things through and realize it. While my own life paralleled Peter's in many ways—we were both senior flight attendants, lived in Chicago, and attended graduate schools—my own career has gone in a different direction. I was looking for a new challenge where I could make a more direct, positive, and more influential impact on people's lives. Recently, I left flying with a traditional major carrier to join an upstart, cutting-edge airline as a Care Specialist, focusing on ways to maintain our company's cohesive connection as we grow and expand. I wanted to make a difference to others, and at the same time, wanted to feel part of a close-knit and caring family. Although I certainly work more hours in my office job and I often miss the time off that flying afforded me, I know this is the right change for me. I love the mental challenge and being an integral part of an organization that values integrity, caring, and fun. Work is an important enough part of my life that I'm glad I found a company culture that fits my personality.

> Between 1990 and 1996, nearly one fifth of all Americans made a voluntary lifestyle change that entailed making less money. Nearly all of them—eighty-five percent—report being happy about the change they made. The most common reason cited for making this kind of life shift is "wanting more time, less stress, and more balance in my life."

# PART-TIME PLOY?

MY TWO FLYING friends, Martha and Dan, and I decided to make the best of a stressful time in our lives. It was March 2003 and war with Iraq appeared inevitable. The winter had seemed particularly long and dreary and the three of us wanted to escape. We quickly packed and went to the airport for that night's departures to Europe.

"I just want to get away," Martha remarked.

"Yes, any city in Europe works for me," Dan added.

"London, full. Paris, full. Rome, not a chance," the gate agent groaned as he stared intently into the computer screen, his hands flying around the keyboard. Then, suddenly, he brightened. "You can get on Amsterdam," he said, "but you'll have to hurry." I looked at the others.

"Let's go," Martha said.

"I'm in," Dan seconded. Laughing, we ran to the gate for final call.

Exhausted after an all-night transatlantic flight, we hopped on the train from Schipol Airport to downtown Amsterdam. From there, we walked to a small, clean hotel recommended by one of the KLM ground officials at the airport. After a few hours of sleep, we awoke to a din from outside our hotel. Startled, we all ran to the window to look out. There we saw an endless crowd, perhaps a half-million people, engulfing the city for as far as the eyes could see. We saw young couples pushing strollers, senior citizens holding signs, and young adults flashing the peace sign. Dan gasped and pointed. An American flag was on fire and we heard the signs of chanting: "Bush is a terrorist! Bush is a terrorist!" Dan, typically animated and outgoing, became suddenly withdrawn. A tear ran down Martha's cheek as she turned away from the window. I gave her a hug. "I don't want the world to hate us," she said.

That night at dinner, Dan started to hyperventilate. He gripped the table and started to rock. As sweat beaded up on his forehead, he blurted out, "My brother had a heart attack and died at my age. Help me."

"Let's go to the hospital," I said, standing up. We darted out of the restaurant and started waving for a cab.

When we arrived at the emergency room, I filled out Dan's paperwork while the nurses took him into a room to get his vital signs. Martha and I joined Dan in the small cubicle while we awaited the doctor's evaluation. Then, the curtain opened and in walked a striking woman in her early thirties with a chic black bob, designer glasses, and a stethoscope over her long white cloak.

"Hello, I'm Doctor Von Dam," she said, smiling, revealing bright, even teeth. "Everything is okay." She put her hand on

Dan's knee and said softly, "It's a difficult time in the world and you are in another country. It's not abnormal to have this kind of reaction."

Dan's lower lip started to quiver and his shoulders slumped. "I am exhausted," he admitted.

The doctor took Dan's hand. "The paperwork here says you are a flight attendant," Dr. Von Dam said.

"We all are," I responded motioning to Martha and myself.

"Me too," the doctor said with a smile as she wrote in the chart. Dan, Martha, and I all exchanged stunned glances.

"KLM, Lead Purser, 737s for Europe," the doctor added casually as she continued to write.

"You mean you were a flight attendant and now you're a doctor?" asked Martha.

The doctor laughed. "No, I am both." Now she really had our attention!

The doctor, whose first name is Henrique, told us that she works two part-time jobs. She works as an emergency-room doctor two days a week and as a flight attendant two days a week, leaving her with plenty of free time. Each job complements the other, she told us.

"My flying job helps me with my people skills and bedside manner in the hospital," she said. "And the intensity of working in the emergency room makes me appreciate the lighter and more upbeat atmosphere of my flying job."

Henrique told us that she has always had an interest in both medicine and traveling. "In my work, I have everything I want," she said simply.

Stopping for a late dinner afterward, we discussed our other interests and why we feel limited to just one career.

"I would love to be a vet," Martha giggled, "and keep flying."

"I like law," Dan added, "though I don't know if I have the patience for school."

Thinking about Henrique's creative work solution, I found myself saying: "I'd like to find something in the airline industry where I can use my clinical social work background," I said out loud. "I'd like to either continue flying and start a private psychotherapy practice or maybe find a clinical job in the airline industry." It was the first time I had spoken aloud about my career fantasy. By saying the words, I started thinking about what kind of career combinations would suit me. And now I have found it. Thank you, Henrique.

According to Peter Meiksins and Peter Whalley, sociology professors at Cleveland State University and Loyola University, Chicago, respectively, Europeans are more inclined to work part-time because of generous mandated government benefits like pensions, government-subsidized college education, and universal health care.

# SLOW DOWN AND SMELL THE GOULASH

DEAN, AN INTERNATIONAL account executive from New York City, met Boris, a Hungarian, while touring Spain. Both were in their midthirties and found they had much in common, from sports to travel.

"You should come visit me in Budapest some time," Boris said.

"Okay, how about next month?" Dean asked.

Boris replied, "Terrific!"

Budapest's beauty surprised Dean. The Danube River divides this picturesque city into two sections, Buda and Pesh. Distinctive cafes and intimate restaurants line the waterway, where Hungarians stroll at their leisure, chat, and bask in their city's natural charm. The ornate baroque architecture of the historic buildings and monuments frame one of Europe's most magnificent cities.

"We're in a fantasyland," Dean exclaimed, drinking in the gingerbread-like domed roofs, minarets, and balconies they encountered with every turn.

"I want to be a good host," Boris said. "What do you want to see and do?"

Dean shrugged, "You call it, Boris."

"Okay, we'll do things that mainstream Hungarians do. Do you like football?" Boris asked.

"I know it as soccer, but yes, I love soccer," replied Dean. They headed for the stadium where a Hungarian team was playing a team from England. By the end of the first quarter, the English were up two to nothing in an apparent rout, yet the local crowd remained energetic and vocal, waving Hungarian flags and frequently breaking into cheers. When the British team scored their third goal, Dean turned to Boris. "It doesn't look good for the home team," he said. "Should we beat traffic and go?"

Boris stared at Dean, baffled. "Why, do you not feel well?" he asked.

A little later, shifting impatiently in his seat, Dean tried again. "We know who is going to win at this point, right?" he asked.

"Ah," Boris smiled and nodded. "I have heard this about Americans."

Dean folded his arms and stared straight ahead. *What had Boris meant by his last comment? Why was his host so intent on wasting his time?*

After the game, Boris and Dean found themselves stalled in traffic for over two hours. Dean kept shifting and twitching in the front seat of the car while Boris made casual conversation.

"Are you okay, Dean?" Boris finally asked.

Dean burst out in frustration: "All this time we've been stuck in a traffic jam, we could have been doing something else."

Boris was quiet for a moment. Then he said: "Dean, you came to visit. We can talk at the game or here in the car or in my apartment or in a café or in a restaurant. The main thing is that two new friends have a chance to know each other. Does it really matter where we are?"

Dean continued to stare straight ahead. Finally he asked, "So what did you hear about Americans?"

Boris laughed. "It is nothing bad, it's just different," he said. "I am sorry if I hurt your feelings. I didn't mean to. It is just that Americans are usually in a hurry and race from place to place—I see the tourists always running from sight to sight on tour buses." He smiled, shaking his head, "Certainly Budapest is beautiful, but the real beauty of our country is in our people. To do nothing special except spend time getting to know our people, understand what we think and why we think it, what it was like to grow up here, under Communist rule, and what it is like now to live day-to-day as a Hungarian—all of this is really the key to understanding and enjoying our culture."

Dean spent the following morning with Boris at one of Budapest's legendary spas. Starting a conversation with the masseuse, he discovered that she hailed from a small town just two hours away from the capital. She shared her dream of opening and owning her own small spa one day. "Now that capitalism has come to Hungary, I have many opportunities," she said to Dean. "What is life like for you in America?"

That afternoon Boris and Dean strolled around the city in a leisurely fashion. Dean began to notice how the slow pace and unplanned approach of the day calmed him. It felt nice to drift! He sat in a café watching the crowd, in particular an elderly couple with deeply lined faces who were talking intently to one another.

"They have some incredible stories to tell," noted Boris. They have witnessed world wars, uprisings, riots, and instability. They are the real Hungarians."

Two hours later, Dean and Boris were still sitting at the café. "What are you thinking?" asked Boris.

"I am thinking how much I am enjoying watching the people, the way they dress, how they treat each other," said Dean reflectively. "I'm just thinking how on the one hand, we are different, but on the other, we're the same. Just thoughts, Boris," he said, his voice trailing off as he scanned the crowd, smiling. "I feel like I am seeing so much more of another country than I ever have before."

John Stilgoe, a history professor at Harvard University, stated on *60 Minutes*, that the power of acute observation is one of nature's most useful tools in learning. The speed of our lives, he contends, leaves little pause for close observation.

# GENEVA GALA

I HAD A few days off and decided to head for Paris. For me, Paris is a magical enclave and I consider it a beautiful and relaxing experience to wander aimlessly past local *patisseries*, listening for the chimes of Notre Dame, and strolling past cuddling couples along the Seine River.

While waiting to go through Immigration and Customs upon arriving at De Gaulle Airport, I met Jennifer, a tall, willowy American woman, graceful and long-legged like a giraffe, who worked for the United Nations and lived in Geneva.

"I overheard you speaking French on the flight—your French is very good," she remarked with a friendly smile.

*"Ah, merrrci bien,"* I responded with my best shot at a "rolling r" Parisian accent. By chance, we were staying at the same hotel and split a taxi downtown. After sharing conversations and laughter in the cab, we both became silent as we approached the Champs d'Elysée and the Arc de Triomphe.

Teary eyed, Jennifer turned to me. "The beauty of this city overwhelms me on every visit," she said.

We decided to meet for dinner that evening. Over plates of cassoulet and a bottle of house cabernet, we traded stories and experiences of living abroad as Americans, speaking "Franglais," in a conversation that used both languages.

"You must visit me in Geneva," Jennifer said, as we capped our dinner with two delicious crème caramels. Comparing calendars, we found a week when we were both free.

"I will throw a dinner party while you're visiting," she promised. "You'll like my friends."

Three evenings after my arrival in crisp, spotless Geneva, dinner guests began to arrive. It was a warm and friendly group, reflecting a mini–United Nations that included guests from Ghana, Brazil, and Algeria. The conversation, mostly in English, spanned several topics—from world politics to new cultural exhibits to travel experiences and future vacation plans.

After the last guest departed well past midnight, I hugged Jennifer. "What a wonderful and stimulating evening, thank you so much!" I said enthusiastically. "But there was one thing I noticed, Jen. Nobody ever talked about their jobs."

Jennifer nodded. "A Swiss friend told me something when I made the same observation upon moving here," she said. "'Europeans, we are multifaceted,' she told me. 'Our jobs are a part of our life, but work talk belongs at work. Work is what we do, it is not who we are.'"

In a study by Professor Ruut Veenhoven, at Eramus University in Rotterdam, Netherlands, entitled the World Database of Happiness, Professor Veenhoven concluded that residents in many European nations are more satisfied with their lives than Americans.

# 3
# Teach Your Children WELL

# AUSTRALIAN VISION

ON OUR THIRD day in Sydney, just after touring the Opera House that overlooks this city filled with waterways and yachts, I accidentally bumped into a dark-haired woman in her late forties. When I immediately apologized, she responded with glee, "You're a Yank!"

"Why, yes, I'm American," I smiled.

"You have to come home with me," she said with a broad, welcoming grin. "My children will be so excited. By the way, my name is Audrey."

Not sure quite how to react, I let her take my arm and we started walking down the street.

"My car is right over there, mate," she chattered, "and I can't tell you how pleased my kids will be. Now the oldest is nineteen . . ."

I looked over my shoulder at my traveling companion, Kirby, and motioned him to catch up with us. "I'm with a friend," I told her, "and we'd been planning to . . ."

She turned us around, approached Kirby, and slid her other arm through his arm. "Then both you boys have to come with me!"

There was something wonderfully disarming about Audrey. She talked nonstop, insisting that Kirby and I not only come meet her husband and children, but also stay for dinner. We hopped in her car and drove toward Audrey's home located in a middle-class subdivision of comfortable homes. Audrey's husband, who had retired a year earlier from his job as a dockworker, had a bushy moustache and a thick middle. Their children, fourteen-year-old Allister and nineteen-year-old Marion, were excited about having us over. After a simple, tasty meal of roast beef and mashed potatoes, Kirby and I answered a slew of questions about New York, San Francisco, Las Vegas, and Miami—the cities the kids wanted to know about.

"What else can we tell you about the States?" I asked as we finished dessert.

"Just keep talking!" Marion suggested, shrugging her shoulders and blushing. "I just like to hear you speak American."

"Thank you so much for coming," Audrey said as she drove us back to the hotel. "It's *so* important for my children to be reminded that there is a whole world outside of Australia."

Kirby and I talked about our experience with Audrey and her family on our flight home.

"I wish I'd grown up in a home that was more welcoming to others," he said. "In particular, it would have been great if I had been exposed to people from other countries as a child."

There are a number of international exchange programs, such as Youth for Understanding, where American families can host an international child or American kids can go overseas and stay with a family.

# FRENCH-CANADIAN RHYTHM

NICK, A FRIEND I played football with when I lived in Greece as a teenager, had the coolest parents. In particular, his mom, Chantal, a good looking French-Canadian woman with a keen sense of humor, kept all the teens entertained. She set limits with her kids when she had to, but on the whole, she gave them as much freedom as possible to grow into young adults. She was fun without being intrusive.

Recently, I heard the family had returned to Canada and since I had a trip planned to Quebec, I decided to look them up. Unfortunately, Chantal's husband, Merlin, had passed away and the kids had moved to western Canada. But Chantal and I agreed to meet for lunch.

Arriving early at the quaint red-shuttered, stone restaurant in the Plaza Royale in Old Quebec City, I asked the owner if I could sit at a table on the flower-lined patio with an unobstructed view of the regal hilltop Chateau Frontenac. Gazing upward, admiring the upright minarets that soared from the sloping green roof of the stone castle, I relaxed in the warmth of the late summer sunshine. The wall in front of the castle appeared to serve as a moat, winding around the chateau and adding to the picturesque, Old World atmosphere.

A few minutes later, a middle-aged woman meandered toward my table. There was no doubt it was Chantal: her trademark dark sunglasses sat atop her coiffed blond bob, framing her delicate features and magenta silk scarf.

"Mrs. C!" I exclaimed, referring to her nickname. As I hugged her and swung her around, we both laughed. We sat down and immediately started reminiscing about days gone by. The waitress came over three times over the next hour to take our order, but we hadn't found a moment to look at the menu.

I told Chantal that I always thought she was a fun mom and that I'd always admired the kind of energy that flowed between her and her kids. She agreed she always had a great rapport with her children, built on trust and honesty.

"Much of how I raised my kids," she reflected, twirling her hair with her finger, "is because of my background."

I asked Chantal what she saw as the biggest difference between her approach and that of the primarily American community they lived among overseas. She hesitated and I sensed she was searching for her words.

"Don't worry about insulting me or my culture," I said with a smile. "Just say it. I can take it—promise!"

Chantal laughed and clasped her hands, finally adding, "Okay."

"I am from Quebec," she said, "and I have been raised to be French." Chantal explained that she noticed how many American parents tried to quickly fix their kids problems instead of her more European approach of listening to her children, empathizing, and letting them work through obstacles on their own.

"It wasn't always easy," Chantal said, "sitting on the sidelines watching my kids make mistakes."

I agreed that it would be difficult to watch children falter.

"Often they would bring up a dilemma," she said, breathing deeply, "and it would take all the energy I had to refrain from giving my opinion. But I knew they would have to stand on their own eventually. So I would say 'That is a tough situation,' and sigh. Then I'd follow up with 'You have a good head on your shoulders. You'll figure out what to do.'"

I nodded and quietly thought about my own parents and their tendency to want to fix our problems—from homework difficulties to friendship woes.

"Letting our children figure it themselves sends several messages," said Chantal. "One, that their father and I trust them to make their own decisions. Two, they learn to trust themselves."

A cross-cultural study by the University of North Carolina at Charlotte found that, in contrast to American parenting styles, European parents treat young adults with respect and expect them to act responsibly.

# FRENCH INTUITION

EDUOARD AND MARTINE, two delightful and loving French friends, came to the United States for vacation. I insisted they stay with me and we were in the midst of an enjoyable week. After making a few calls to friends, I arranged dinner plans at one of my favorite local restaurants.

We had just been seated at a table for eight near the main entrance of the restaurant when a couple entered with their young daughter. The girl appeared to be about six years old and was wearing an adorable outfit, complete with a matching red beret and shawl. Martine leaped out of her seat and leaning over, walked toward the little girl until they were eye-to-eye.

"You are 'byootiful,'" she said while clutching her hands over her heart. The little girl started to giggle, shrug, and murmured "thank you."

Then her mother pulled her daughter away and guided her toward a table on the other side of the restaurant. The mother then pointed her finger at her daughter and scolded, "I told you never to talk to strangers."

Martine returned to the table with tears in her eyes. "It's because I am French, no?" she asked.

"No, Martine," I said softly, rubbing her shoulder. "She is trying to protect her daughter." I explained the American approach of shielding children from possible predators.

"That's crazy," Martine said, emphatically pulling her napkin across her lap. I decided to call her on it.

"Then how did you teach your son to react to strangers?" I asked.

Martine explained that children are intuitive and she taught her son to trust his intuition. "If he feels uncomfortable, then he finds a way to leave," she said.

Eduoard agreed. "We believe that most people are good, loving people and we taught Robert that," he said. There was silence at the table. "If we taught our children to be scared and not talk to people, how would they develop a belief in humanity?"

I silently nodded. That night I tossed and turned thinking about the evening. *What kind of messages are we sending our kids? Is our fear of others turning us into a callous and disconnected nation?*

According to the National Center for Missing or Exploited Children, children are better served with instructions to be wary of certain kinds of situations or behaviors rather than by instructions to be wary of individuals with an unusual or disheveled appearance.

# ARGENTINE ATTRIBUTES

BEFORE ARRIVING IN Buenos Aires, all I knew about Maria was that she was thirty-one years old, divorced, and had two kids under the age of ten. Maria was a friend of Dave and Kathy, two friends of mine from New York who encouraged me to look her up during my visit. "You will love her," they promised.

Maria and I agreed to meet in front of the hotel. She pulled up fifteen minutes late, which I would learn is actually early in Argentina. When she leaped out of her car, I saw a smiling woman with black hair flipped up at the ends like Marlo Thomas. She was actually petite, but her spiky pumps made her look taller and her bright green sweater tied around her neck over her black dress gave her an air of sophistication. Her arms open, she graciously kissed me on both cheeks.

"*Hola* Bill," she said warmly. Instantly, I liked her.

We drove down the wide boulevards of Buenos Aires with shops lining the sides of the eight-lane thoroughfares. Well-dressed shoppers carrying designer bags crowded the sidewalks. As we drove past the Royal Palace with its brilliant orange and pink hues, Maria pointed out the balcony where

Eva Peron stood to address the people. We went to a chic restaurant near the Royal Palace for lunch.

"If you like beef, you must order the *lomo,*" Maria suggested. I did so and as I feasted on the most tender piece of steak I'd ever eaten (which, by the way, did not require a knife), we began to get to know each other.

Maria told me how she married her first love at nineteen. "Young," she said shaking her head, "and stupid." Although there had been trouble in the relationship from the beginning, she thought that having a child would help them as a couple.

"But Julio and I grew even further apart," she recalled. "Out of loneliness, I decided to have another child." The marriage continued to deteriorate, and Maria and Julio decided to divorce.

The good news, Maria said, is that she and Julio have agreed to focus on what is best for their children.

"The divorce is between him and me," Maria explained. "We knew it would be hard enough on the kids, so we decided to finally act like adults!" They established some rules: they would never speak poorly of each other to their children or to friends or relatives, they would not allow the children to speak poorly of either of them, and they would always treat each other warmly and politely in their children's company.

Equally important, they agreed to make the children a priority in their lives, and to take the time each week to talk with each other about their children's activities and how they can support their interests.

"It's worked out so well that I actually might be falling back in love with him," Maria confessed. "Julio is a wonderful dad and that is warming my heart."

Findings from the National Longitudinal Study of Adolescent Health suggest that "parental connectedness" is the single biggest factor in protecting adolescents from such risks as school failure, pregnancy, and substance abuse.

# ENGLISH MANNERS

I MET ABBY, a British friend, for lunch in Manhattan. A tall woman with green eyes and short, sassy auburn hair, Abby is known for her bright smile and quick wit. Over soup and salad, I asked her what she perceived to be the biggest difference between our cultures on either side of the "big pond." Without missing a beat, she said: "Our table manners."

Horrified, I put down my knife and fork. Abby tilted her head back and roared.

"Not *you* in particular," she chuckled. "But some of you in the colonies need a refresher course in proper eating," she grinned. "And especially the children here," she went on, shaking her head. "Parents need to find the time to teach their kids the basics."

With a nervous laugh, I cautiously picked up my fork. Trying not to be obvious, I watched Abby expertly dip her spoon into her soup and ladle away from herself. I noticed how she sliced and ate her salad with her fork upside down in her left hand, while ably wielding her knife in her right hand. Taking small bites, she was somehow able to carry an animated conversation without food in her mouth.

"I can tell a lot about where someone was raised by having a meal with them," Abby observed. "And in England," she continued playfully, tilting her head to the side, "We are *very* into being 'propah.'" We both laughed.

After the meal, I thought about what I'd learned about table manners growing up. We had dinner every night at the dining-room table and my parents modeled proper eating rituals. My brothers and I received gentle reminders like "please, no elbows on the table," or "smaller bites please." Although the basics were instilled from a young age, there are times that I become lax and lazy. Abby taught me to be more conscientious; in public, at home, and with my family. As a result of Abby's cultural observation, I make a concerted effort to model proper manners for my niece and nephew. Refined table manners are a sign of being well-bred and those kinds of touches will serve them well in their personal and professional lives.

> "On the continent, people have good food; in England people have good table manners." —George Mikes, British author

# NICARAGUAN KNOW-HOW

EMMA, MY BRIGHT, lively thirty-five-year-old Nicaraguan neighbor in Forest Hills, met Don, her American husband, twelve years ago at a government gala in the capital of Managua, where he was stationed with the U.S. Embassy. They quickly married and three years later their son Don Jr. was born. Sadly, they have not lived happily ever after. When the couple divorced two years ago, Emma contemplated returning to Nicaragua with her son.

Over a second cup of coffee one Saturday morning, Emma shared her experience.

"My thoughts about returning to Nicaragua had nothing to do with punishing my ex-husband with finances," Emma explained. "Don and I had an amicable divorce, and money is not a problem. It had to do with what I saw as a proper parenting role and the priorities I wanted to instill in Don Jr." She explained that she didn't like the competitive qualities her nine-year-old was adopting and she refused to buy him the endless range of toys to keep up with his private-school friends. Although returning to Nicaragua would have been an easy alternative, she didn't want to take her son so far from his father.

"So," Emma continued, "I decided to re-create the Nicaraguan way of life here." Emma went to the PTA meeting at her son's school, raised her hand and made her points.

"I told them about my background, my concerns about my son, and the traits I am looking for in my child's peers," she recalled. "Then I asked for parents who shared the same thoughts to contact me after the meeting." After the meeting, Emma was surrounded by parents. Together with the other interested parents, they organized their own visits to local parks, zoos, and libraries. One of the fathers organized a group hike and another mother invited the group over to bake and ice a cake. Soon Emma and Don Jr. had built their own community within a community. Emma smiled as she sipped.

"I found concerned parents with nice kids who were looking to spend more time with each other," she said. "Creating an atmosphere to get Don Jr. back on track," she said as she swirled her coffee cup, "is my single greatest accomplishment."

A nationwide poll of U.S. children, commissioned by the Center for a New American Dream, found that ninety percent of kids ages nine to fourteen say friends and family are "way more important" than things that money can buy. Additionally, a Gallup Youth Survey of high school students found that two-thirds of the teens reported that they wished they could spend more time with their parents.

# TOKYO TODDLERS

I HAD JUST settled into my aisle seat for the fourteen-hour flight from New York to Tokyo. Coming toward me down the aisle was a Japanese family of four—two parents in their mid-thirties and their two daughters, about four and two years old. The middle row across the aisle from me, which held five seats, was open. *"Please stop at another row farther back,"* I thought to myself as the family approached my row. But the father, holding a small tote bag with a doll's head and a stuffed monkey poking out of the top, stopped next to me, and signaled for his family to enter the row. My lips tightened. Burying my head in my carry-on, I searched feverishly for my ear plugs and sighed with relief upon discovering them.

However, to my delight, I never needed them. The girls were seated between their parents and I noticed the adults' movements were particularly slow and deliberate. The children seemed to reflect their parents' calm demeanor and appeared relaxed in their seats, quietly lost in thought. Both parents were always in physical contact with their kids, lightly holding one daughter's hand or placing an arm around the other child's shoulder.

The younger girl pointed to the stuffed monkey and looked up at her father with a smile. As she whispered something to him, he put his ear down to her mouth to hear her better. As he listened, he smiled and nodded, slowly taking the monkey out of the bag and placing the toy in his daughter's lap. She brought the monkey up to her shoulder and rocked it like a baby.

Meanwhile, the older girl reached for the safety card in the seat pocket and pulled on it, causing a slight tear. Her mother calmly reached for the card and after gently taking it out of the child's hand, she carefully put the card back in the seat pocket. The girl looked up at her mother. Her mother slowly shook her head back and forth and took her daughter's hand. They gazed into each other's eyes and smiled while their clasped hands gently rocked together. The young girl leaned against her mother's arm and closed her eyes.

After lunch, the family went to sleep. The two girls leaned up against their mother while the father rested between his daughters with his arms over one daughter's legs and the other daughter's legs touching his back.

When the family woke, they quietly played together with the stuffed animals. The girls quietly stifled giggles and the foursome smiled and played house. It was one of the quietest, most relaxing and peaceful flights I have ever enjoyed.

In a 1996 study comparing Japanese and American parenting styles, social researchers William Caudill and Helen Weinstein found that although there was no difference in the amount of time mothers talked and played with their kids, the quality of the interaction differed. Japanese mothers spoke more soothingly to their children and spent more time in bodily contact with them, resulting in calmer and seemingly more content children.

# THIRD WORLD TOUCHES

DIMITRA AND I were hiking above the clouds in the Andes, looking down the green-sloped mountain at the mass of workers picking vegetables. From a distance, we couldn't figure out why many of the workers were wearing slings.

"Surely, they can't all be hurt," Dimitra noted.

"Perhaps the slings are contraptions to hold the day's harvest," I proposed.

Later that day I asked the owner of our lodge about the slings. We learned that almost all of these women wore "*chalenas*" or slinglike contraptions, on their backs to carry their children. The next day Dimitra and I went on a hike and ventured closer to the workers. A young woman who had been diligently picking berries suddenly stopped. Swinging her sling to the front of her body, she gathered it up to her breast and began to breast-feed her infant. After a couple of minutes, she carefully swung the sling around onto her back, wiped her breast with her shirt and resumed picking.

I asked Laura, a vivacious twenty-six-year-old American Peace Corps volunteer who was staying at our lodge, what she knew about the slings. Laura was completing the second year of her mission in Ecuador.

"Birth control is rare here," she explained, "and most women are faced with the dilemma of raising several children while needing to work." She explained how the sling or "*chalena*" allows moms to remain physically and emotionally connected to their infants at all times. "That's why kids are so happy here. Notice that you rarely hear them crying."

Dimitra and I looked at each other and smiled. A few days earlier we'd discussed how content the children seemed in Ecuador. We noticed this not just on the crowded flight to Quito, but also on the scores of local buses loaded with families. The kids quietly sat on their parents' laps or sat next to their parents, holding their hands.

> According to researchers Lozoff and Brittenham, babies in the United States are in physical contact with their parents about half as frequently as babies in third-world societies.

# FILIPINO OPTIMISM

MY EXPERIENCE IN Ecuador reminded me of my experience in the Philippines. I was visiting a friend, Jerry, a cultural specialist and psychologist I met in graduate school who is now doing contract work for the U.S. government. After a brisk walk through Rizal Park in the historical part of Manila, Jerry and I hopped on a bus to check out some of the local markets. On the way, the ancient bus, billowing blue smoke from the exhaust, came to a complete standstill. We were in the midst of a neighborhood and as I looked out the window, I peered right into the bedroom of a home. The curtains were partly open and I saw a family of four—two parents and two toddlers—asleep in the same large bed. *Strange,* I thought to myself. The house looked large and certainly enough room for separate sleeping quarters.

"Jerry, look," I said pointing to the sleeping family. "They all sleep with each other," he said. I grimaced with alarm.

"That is such an American reaction," Jerry scolded. "It's normal for Filipino children to *appropriately* sleep with their parents, sometimes until they are teenagers."

But that was not the most interesting part of child rearing

in the Philippines. Jerry elaborated by telling me how Filipino parents teach their children the cultural norm of refraining from negative comments and to maintain cordial relations with others.

"Parents focus on the positive with a great result," Jerry said. "Filipino kids grow up thinking the glass is always half full, they have the support of their family and they are some of the happiest kids I have ever seen."

"Look at those kids," Jerry said, pointing to a group of children on a playground. We watched a young teen help a younger girl, who had fallen, back up on her feet. A few minutes later we saw a young girl help a child with special needs go down a slide. Jerry turned to me and said, "When you raise kids to be optimistic, they are more helpful and less judgmental."

> If you have nothing nice to say, say nothing at all.

# LEBANESE CONNECTION

ON THE RIDE from the airport through Beirut, the "Paris of the Middle East," Katie and Simon, family friends and my hosts, took me on a unique route. As we drove along the Mediterranean, we passed Lebanese couples and families strolling along the *"roche"* or boardwalk. To my right were large condominiums overlooking the Mediterranean, and to my left, Pigeon Rock, a huge natural rock formation with hundreds of pigeons flapping around their turf. The city was a series of contrasts, with shiny, recently constructed office towers next to dilapidated old tenements and a slew of buildings under construction. It took me awhile to get used to the sight of bombed buildings and memorial sights, but the optimism of the people and their passion for life allowed me to envision a wonderful future for the Lebanese.

Katie, Simon, their two daughters (seventeen-year-old Huda and fourteen-year-old Muna), and I went skiing for the day. Amazingly, we left the Mediterranean warmth of Beirut and a little over an hour later, we were in the mountains, ankle deep in snow, getting in line for the lifts. Simon had an incredible rapport with his daughters. He adored them and told them so repeatedly. Muna and I rode the chairlift together and I commented about her relationship with her dad.

"He is the best," she said. "I feel like I can tell him anything."

Two runs later, Huda and I were on the chairlift together. I shared with her how much I appreciated her family and enjoyed her parents. Huda told me how she started to pull away from her parents a couple years ago. She recalled her father sitting down with her one evening.

"He explained that my pulling away was normal for a teenager," she said with a smile. "Then he told me he would give me all the space I needed," she recalled with a laugh. "But he told me to always remember that I will always be his girl and I can go to him with any problem at any time."

A tear ran down Huda's face. I silently took her hand and gave it a squeeze. We looked at each other and smiled.

According to Joe Kelly, president of the nonprofit advocacy group Dads & Daughters, daughters often feel rejected and alienated if their dads back away from them in adolescence.

# SALVADOR SOLACE

My friend Cindy is a flight attendant in her midforties, with auburn hair and a broad smile. When her children grew up and left home, she realized that she wanted to do something to make the world a better place. She volunteered with a group of airline employees for a mission to visit orphaned children in El Salvador.

The first stop on the mission was an orphanage for HIV-positive babies. Cindy saw ten full cribs lined up against the wall, each with three babies. Three caretakers frantically scurried around the room trying to feed and change the group. One lone, unmarked jar of Vaseline stood on a stool with a single Popsicle stick sticking out of the top. Cindy immediately jumped in and started changing crying babies.

"I couldn't help but notice that each baby had no reaction to touch," Cindy said, wondering if it was the effects of the disease. When she was told the babies had no reaction because there was no time for the caretakers to hold or rock the babies, Cindy's eyes filled with tears. She picked up a tiny girl in her arms and rocked her, wishing she could take her home.

The next stop on the route was an orphanage for children with cerebral palsy. Cindy walked into the orphanage and locked eyes with a thirteen-year-old boy seated in a dilapidated wheelchair.

She knelt down and said, "We brought you a new wheelchair."

Although the child spoke no English, he reached out and wrapped his arms around Cindy and rocked her back and forth.

"That was the magic moment for me," she said. "I knew at that point I had found my calling. My own kids may be grown up and gone, but I will always be a mom."

Cindy now organizes regular missions for JetBlue volunteers. This January, we are filling an aircraft with donated hospital and school supplies, hygiene items and toys for children, and flying to El Salvador on a six-day mission. I am so excited to be a part of this group. On our trip, we will deliver love and supplies to the children at San Rafael Hospital, decorate a home for unwed mothers, deliver school supplies to children on coffee plantations, and take one hundred underprivileged children on their first airplane flight!

According to a study by the Touch Research Institute at the University of Miami, premature infants who were massaged were more active, more alert, and matured forty-seven percent faster in terms of motor development than those infants who did not receive massage.

# SPANISH CREATIVITY

ON A RECENT trip to Spain, I found the city of Barcelona sophisticated and enchanting. As I left my hotel, heading downhill to the port, I looked back at the bustling streets that wound up a series of picturesque hills. The streets were lined with ornate buildings, most featuring wrought-iron balconies filled with flowers. As I entered the port area, I saw a number of small yachts bobbing in the water under the warm and comfortable Mediterranean sun.

After taking a brisk walk, I opted for a different route back to the hotel and cut through a park. The manicured flower beds, bursting with purple and red flowers, were so captivating that I decided to take a seat on a bench and take it all in. I noticed a woman in her midthirties, dressed simply in jeans and a crisp white T-shirt with a floral scarf tied smartly around her neck. She was sitting on a park bench with her arm around her daughter, who was about eight years old and wearing a ponytail, as the child sat with a drawing board on her lap. The mother gently scanned the sky, pointing at the puffy clouds. She then stood and walked toward the flower bed directly across from them, motioning at the yellow flowers. The young girl smiled and enthusiastically started to draw. The mother returned to the bench and continued with words of encouragement, "*Bueno, bueno,* Margarite."

Margarite squealed with delight as her mother continued to point out different sights with a series of "oohs," "ahs," and "*Si* Margarite."

A man appearing to be Margarite's father walked toward them with a tray of refreshments. He joined the duo and immediately started admiring the drawing. He hugged his daughter, took the drawing and placed it over his heart. Margarite giggled and jumped into her father's arms while her mother laughed. The threesome, hand-in-hand, with Margarite skipping in the middle, made their way toward the park exit.

| |
|---|
| A 2002 study concluded that as a result of more time to discover and explore their interior life, European children exhibit more imagination and creativity than American children. Furthermore, the study found that American kids are more likely to be insecure and depressed than kids in Brazil, China, Germany, India, Japan, and Spain. |

# IT TAKES A VILLAGE

PIRKO, A TALL, slim Finnish woman with a broad smile, is a friend of a friend. I called Pirko when I found myself connecting through Helsinki on my way to the Baltic country of Estonia. Pirko met me at the hotel and whisked me to Olympic Stadium. Approaching the modern arena, I could see the series of Olympic rings and a huge multitiered stadium.

Pirko said, "Wait till you see the view from the tower."

Unfortunately, the fog was thick that day, which obstructed the view of the city. However, the open arena was tranquil and provided a comfortable venue for Pirko and I to talk.

"The complex is modern by today's standards and certainly must have been perceived as cutting edge in 1940, when it was built," Pirko proudly said. "It is known as the most beautiful Olympic village in the world."

"I wish I had more than a day," I remarked. "I'd love to get a feel for the Finnish culture, see where you live, meet your kids."

She had told me earlier that she had three children. She smiled. "They are with my other family,' she responded.

"Your other family—what is that?" I asked.

As we sat in the arena and looked out at the empty track below, Pirko described how she and her neighbors work together to raise their children. She found four other neighborhood families she trusts and who share similar child-rearing styles.

"As Finns, we are trusting and accepting," Pirko said. "The most important thing is to accept each child as they are and support them in their interests." Pirko explained that all of the parents in the group have agreed to support all of the neighborhood kids' interests, regardless of whether they share the interest themselves.

"When it comes to kids, you get what you get," Pirko shrugged. "They have to know their individual passions are important and supported." She laughed. "Ursula's son, Stefan, loves the piano," she said. Placing her palms upward, she continued. "And, of course, I know nothing about the piano—my son loves soccer and it took me forever to understand that game!" "But," she sighed, "it is not about what interests me. Although Stefan isn't really my son, I am learning about the piano!"

Each month, Pirko said, the parents meet to make sure they are on the same page.

"It sounds almost perfect," I noted.

Pirko laughed. "No, actually this month, for the first time in years, we had trouble agreeing."

Pirko described the split among the parents about computer usage. Some thought it could be very educational while others believed it kept their children from being active. The parents do their homework and present their findings at the monthly meetings.

"Ironically enough, we did our homework on the Internet!" Pirko chuckled.

Pirko discovered that almost three quarters of American kids regularly use the Internet—the highest in the world—versus an average Internet use of a little less than half the kids in Finland.

"I know about the obesity problem American kids are facing," Pirko said. "And I knew I didn't want our kids sitting in front of a computer and becoming inactive."

"After a spirited debate, active won out," Pirko exclaimed. "The group agreed to limit the amount of time on the Internet. Now the kids can only use the computer at Ursula's house on Tuesdays."

As I sat processing all of this, I reflected on Hillary Clinton's book, *It Takes a Village*. "What would have happened if you couldn't agree?" I asked.

Pirko stared straight ahead, seemingly lost in thought. "I guess we would have broken up the group and aligned ourselves with other families who saw things the way we do." Pirko responded. But she explained that there is generally room for negotiation.

"Thankfully, we are flexible and reasonably logical," she said.

One of the best things about the group, said Pirko, is that

the children have all become close and consider each other siblings.

"Of course, some are closer than others," Pirko noted. "However, they are all good to each other." Each mom in the neighborhood takes a day to be responsible for all the kids, allowing the other parents some time to visit museums or go to lunch with a friend.

"Most importantly, I know they are safe and in a supportive and forgiving environment. I can give up control and have some time for me," Pirko said. "And that makes me a better mother!"

United we stand, divided we fall.

# SETTING LIMITS, SHOWING LOVE

LULY AND XAVIER are first generation Cuban friends in their early forties who live outside Miami. Although both speak English fluently, they speak Spanish at home and are closely linked with Cuban traditions. When I visited them in Miami, we went to a small café for coffee in Little Havana.

Luly and Xavier have two teenage daughters, Marcella and Sylvia, who had just gone through a rebellious stage.

Luly said, "They were starting to fall in with the wrong crowd. The girls started to dress more seductively and took on an edge."

Xavier shook his head and described how the girls suddenly became surly with Luly. "I couldn't talk to them either," he said, shrugging his shoulders. "I didn't know where my sweet girls went."

By working long hours, Luly and Xavier had been able to buy a nice home in Coral Gables.

"Xavier and I looked around at our nice things and realized they meant nothing without our girls," Luly said. "My gut feeling told me to do something—and do it fast." She spoke to her boss and began to work from home. She also cut her hours to part-time.

Then they arranged a family meeting. "Xavier and I tried to speak with one voice," Luly recalled. "The girls fought us, they yelled and screamed, but we stood our ground and set down rules and strict curfews."

Xavier nodded somberly. "It was a tough road. After one particularly heated battle, I found Luly in our bedroom sobbing."

Luly's eyes started to tear and she said, "I thought they might run away and we would lose them, but Xavier gave me the strength to carry on. He hugged me a lot that night, and by the next day I was back on track."

The next morning, Luly told the girls at breakfast that she and Xavier were laying down the law because they loved them. "Yes, I remember that day," Xavier said. "I think we turned the corner that morning." The girls were quiet and listened. As they spoke of this turning point, they instinctively held hands.

"We took weekend trips together as a family, to the beach or fishing," said Luly. "I started taking them out individually or together for lunch and just talking."

"At the beginning, I did most of the talking!" she added with a smile. The time was well spent for Luly. She realized she didn't know her girls as well as she thought.

"Finally, the girls came around and we started to really talk." Luly sighed. Luly realized the girls were feeling neglected.

"The girls just needed our time and attention," Xavier concluded.

According to a 2002 poll commissioned by the Center for a New American Dream, nearly one in four U.S. teens say their parents are too busy at work. Nearly two-thirds of the teens said that, if granted only one wish, they would want their parents to have a job that gave them more time to do fun things together as a family.

# IT'S ONLY NATURAL

MY BUS HAD just pulled out of the charming capital of Tallinn, Estonia, heading to the rural city of Parnu. Estonia is a Baltic country that once was occupied by Russia. I smiled at the young woman across the aisle as she settled into her seat with her infant.

"Very cute," I said nodding to her child.

She returned the smile. "My English," she said haltingly and then took her free hand and waved it back and forth.

"And my Estonian," I responded. "BAD!" I added emphatically. We both laughed.

"Where you are from?" she asked me casually, exposing her breast and placing her nipple in her child's mouth without losing eye contact with me.

"Huh?" I responded, feeling my face turn red.

"You, you America? Canada?" she asked. I didn't dare look down. Nobody else on the bus seemed to care that this woman was openly breast-feeding.

A year later I was in the middle seat on a flight between Athens and Frankfurt. The woman in the window seat, without the benefit of a blanket, started to breast-feed her infant. Shortly thereafter, when I was in Costa Rica, I saw a woman do the same in the hotel lobby. Upon returning to the United States, I called a sociologist friend.

"What's up with all these women breast-feeding in public?" I asked.

"By your tone," she responded, "I have to wonder who has the issue?"

She explained that breast-feeding is common all around the world. "It's the most natural and healthy act in the world," she said. "Women invented formula."

"But," I countered, "do they have to breast-feed in public? And if so, don't you think they should cover up?"

"They feed when the baby is hungry," she responded curtly. "And if *you* are uptight about nudity, then don't look."

I thought about it and realized that she is right—I was the one with the hang up. Now, in my travels, when I see a mother openly breast-feeding, which is often—I smile and nod!

According to researchers Morrow and Tlucak, babies and children who were breast-fed as infants score higher on cognitive tests than those who received formula. UNICEF and the World Health Organization have declared breast-feeding as the healthiest way to feed babies, because it protects against infections. The National Institute of Environmental Health and Safety estimates that four out of every thousand infants in the United States die because they are not breast-fed.

# 4
# To Your HEALTH

# DUTCH TREAT

ON MY FIRST trip to Amsterdam as a crew member, a gregarious Dutch passenger named Gunther ambled to the back galley to purchase duty-free items on the late-night transatlantic flight. After entertaining the crew with jokes and stories, he offered to take the flight attendants on a tour of Amsterdam upon our arrival. I pictured us zooming around in a sporty, late-model European car, taking in the sights of this famously picturesque city. Though the rest of the crew had other plans, I eagerly took Gunther up on his offer and arranged to meet him downtown the following day.

When I arrived the next morning at our designated meeting spot, Gunther was already waiting for me, accompanied by two shy, attractive young women. After exchanging pleasantries, the four of us made our way toward an enormous, multilevel parking garage adjacent to Amsterdam's main train station. To my amazement, there were no cars in the garage. Instead, I saw bicycles—thousands and thousands of them! Gunther pointed to a bike for me, and the four of us rode off on a leisurely tour of Amsterdam. We pedaled past tall, narrow row homes in a stunning array of colors, from pastel peach to moss green to deep ochre. Turning a corner, we rode past ornate churches, redbrick shops, and a series of bed-and-breakfasts lining a charming canal. As I cycled through the pristine, regal city, I realized that had we traveled by car, I would have noticed only a fraction of the intriguing sights, sounds, and smells that greeted me on two wheels. Nor would I have gotten the invigorating exercise provided by a self-propelled mode of transportation! By the time we stopped at a café for lunch, I felt more alive and energetic than I had in weeks.

The four of us sat outside the café under a white canopy, sipping sparkling water and watching the parade of activity. It was the first time I got a good look at the city's most popular mode of transportation. Most bicycles are simple, gearless, and somewhat battered.

As Gunther explained in his halting English, "Our bikes are the same as the people. We Dutch don't like flash."

Every day, rain or shine (and it's often rain), thousands of people take to the streets, crowding the designated bike paths on main thoroughfares and crisscrossing the small inlets that weave through the city. Among the cyclists I saw were couples in their seventies, moms with their kids, and business people balancing briefcases.

The city is literally a swarm of bike riders holding hands, carrying umbrellas, and eating while transporting themselves around town. Biking is not just an urban ritual; it's a way of life. The result of this cycling mania: the Dutch are noticeably fit and lean. During an entire day of cycling the city and passing thousands of people, I spotted maybe five individuals whom I would call heavy.

According to the Dutch Tourist Bureau, cycling is the main form of transportation in Holland—there are actually more bikes in the country than people. Additionally, cycling is so popular that the Dutch Parliament employs its own bicycle repair staff, and at one university, there is actually a professor of cycling!

# TURKISH BATH

ARRIVING AT ISTANBUL in the late morning allowed me to arrange a quick afternoon tour of the city—the only one in the world built on two continents. From my hotel, I could see the palace on top of the hill with towering minarets on each side. First, I hopped in a cab to the majestic Topkapi Palace, and then the driver swung me over to the azure-tiled Blue Mosque. From there, I walked to the Hippodrome, the most important stadium of ancient times. After a busy afternoon, I checked into my hotel on the European side of the Bosporus, the waterway that separates Europe and Asia.

Seeking relaxation at the end of the day, I asked the concierge to direct me to the nearest *hamam,* or traditional Turkish bath. Good news: there was one right around the corner. I walked through the glass entry doors of the tall, domed building where a man sat behind a counter flanked by a list of what appeared to be prices and services written on a chalkboard. He led me to a small room lined with lockers and gave me a sarong and a key with an elastic band to keep around my wrist. Wrapping the red-and-white-checked cotton sarong around my waist, I proceeded down the stairs toward the main spa area.

Walking under an arch, I entered a massive marble room, where I saw a flat, round marble slab in the center, surrounded by several small cubicles featuring private washbasins and showers. Habib, the masseur, clad in a matching sarong, motioned me toward the sauna in the corner of the room. Opening its door, I was nearly overcome by the intensity of the heat. (Later, I found out that the temperature is set to 130 degrees!) After about ten minutes, when sweat was pouring out of my every pore, Habib opened the door and motioned me out. As I thirstily gulped mineral water that was waiting for me on a side table, Habib smiled and said "good, good." He then signaled for me to climb onto the marble slab and lie on my back. With no further ado, he doused me with hot water and started to scrub my body with a rough cloth. Every stroke hurt, but I wanted to get the full effect, so I bit my lower lip and endured. After scrubbing my entire body, Habib signaled for me to shower. It was then that I noticed that my body was covered with hundreds of tiny flakes. It was my skin! I had been completely exfoliated.

After I showered, Habib doused me again, this time with an unnamed sudsy solution. For a solid hour, he twisted, stretched, cracked, straddled, and manipulated my body until I was completely limp. The price: ten million Turkish lira, or about six dollars. I have never been, or felt, so completely cleansed. My entire body glowed. That night, I slept heavily for almost eleven hours. When I awoke, I felt stretched, long and lean—and more than ready for a full day of getting to know Istanbul.

*Hamams* are either strictly for men or women; however, many *hamams* cater to both sexes, offering specific days for either men or women.

# MAGICAL MADEIRA

I HAD A chunk of vacation time coming up the following month, but without a hefty cash reserve, I wasn't sure I could squeeze a trip out of the opportunity. In the midst of my deliberations, a friend called me and asked me to join her on a two-week cruise across the Atlantic from Fort Lauderdale to Barcelona. Better yet, the price was right because the trip was a relocation cruise (when cruise lines transition ships from one part of the world to another). I jumped at the chance.

When the horn blew at seven AM, I leaped out of bed realizing that we were finally pulling into a port after five straight days on the water. We were halfway through the two-week jaunt "across the big pond" and had only stopped once for a brief visit in Bermuda. Stepping onto the balcony, I rubbed my eyes and tried to focus as the first glimmer of sun rose on the horizon. Directly in front of me was a magnificent island with rolling green hills, covered by dazzling bright pink, yellow, and purple flowers. A scattering of villalike homes with large terraces jutted out from the hillside, overlooking the hustle and bustle of the small port town. The narrow streets wove and wound aimlessly up the steep incline, disappearing over the hilltops.

After I showered and dressed, I quickly scampered down the gangplank and off the ship, not wanting to miss a minute of my precious twelve hours in Madeira. The year-round spring-like warmth of the Mediterranean sun wrapped me in a soft, cozy glow, like a light feather comforter. I stood in the middle of town and looked up at the sharp embankment, where crowds of people were briskly trekking downward through narrow walkways. Businessmen and women, toting briefcases, tilted their bodies slightly backward to maintain balance as they expertly maneuvered down the steep embankment on their way to work. A smattering of families, their arms loaded with fresh fruits and vegetables, headed in the other direction up the hill. Not understanding Portuguese, I simply enjoyed the soft "jush" of the language that surrounded me, almost as though everybody was lisping. One of several small cars was trying to make its way up the hill, but had no choice but to keep pace with the crowd. It seemed like everybody on this small island was in port and nearly all of them were walking!

When I found an opening in the crowd, I darted across the street to a café. There I found an empty table and sat down, my eyes now level with the torsos of hundreds of locals. Sipping a cup of strong Portuguese coffee, I found myself thinking, *I've never seen a population with such well-developed calves!*

Afterward, I stood at the bottom of the street once more and looked up at a ninety-degree angle. What appeared to be a manageable hill from the tenth deck of the ship an hour earlier now looked like a daunting mountain. *"Just do it,"* I said to myself and off I went. I fell into step behind an elderly couple who were charging up the hill arm-in-arm, the woman wearing a dress and shoes with low, chunky heels, while her companion wore a gray suit and black loafers. I was wearing walking shorts and sneakers. *If they can do it,* I thought, *so can I!*

The first thirty minutes of the climb were blissful. I passed beautiful, gated villas, their rambling yards filled with trees loaded down with sun-kissed lemons, bright oranges, and ripe figs. Then my breathing became labored and the sweat started to trickle down my face. Forty-five minutes up the hill, my easy trot slowed to a stumble as I put my hand on top of my thigh to brace myself for each additional step. The older couple, amicably chit-chatting, grew gradually smaller in the distance as they turned yet another winding corner up the hill and out of sight. Stepping to the side of the road, with my hands on my hips, I caught my breath and turned to survey the island from another perspective. I gasped again—but not from exhaustion. Instead, I marveled at the sight before me—a vision of flowers, fruits, trees, sunlight, and greenery. I experienced a moment of total serenity, surrounded by the best that nature had to offer.

At that moment I decided to incorporate hiking into my life. Although I regularly used the Stairmaster at the gym, this was a different kind of workout—with very different rewards. Upon my return home, I discovered a park near my house with a variety of trails and small hills. In addition, on vacations, I began to seek a number of different physical challenges—including a seven-hour climb up Mount Villarica in Chile and a ten-mile hike around Crystal Lake in Ecuador. I still work out at the gym, but I now "spice up" my fitness regimen with lots of outdoor activities.

According to *Men's Fitness,* "shocking" our muscles with a variety of exercises is the best way to stay in shape. Our bodies readily adjust to the same form of exercise, thereby decreasing its strengthening and toning.

# ISLAND INSPIRATION

I PUT THE power—and pleasure—of "active living" to the test on a recent visit to the Caribbean island of Saint Martin. A family from Corsica occupied the room next door to me at a small, quaint inn near the town of Marigot, on the French side of the island. Each morning, on my way to the beach, I passed the family in my rental car. They were animated and laughing, obviously enjoying each other's company as they strolled to the same beach where I was headed. As I sped by them, I was stunned to realize that I had never even *thought* about getting to the beach on my own steam, even though it was only about a mile away. What was my rush?

The next morning, I walked to the beach, listening to parakeets chattering in the trees and admiring the crimson hibiscus plants on my way. For the remainder of the week, I walked back and forth to the beach every day, enjoying the feel of my limbs waking up as I breathed in the local sights and sounds. In the evenings, I joined the throngs of European tourists meandering through the streets and exploring the charming island. My rental car sat in front of the hotel, all but abandoned.

When I returned home, I began to integrate walking into my daily life. Fortunately, I live within walking distance to work, so I start and finish my workday with a brisk twenty-minute walk in each direction. In addition, I try to incorporate different forms of cardio exercise into my daily life. In addition to cycling and walking, I play tennis and take kickboxing classes. I also practice yoga to relax and "recenter" myself after a busy day.

According to the latest studies from the National Institutes of Health, just a half hour of brisk walking on most days of the week will substantially reduce your risk of heart disease, diabetes, high blood pressure, and a host of other serious disorders. It also does wonders for the waistline. An hour-long walk around the neighborhood at three miles per hour burns 320 calories, while a more serious "exercise" walk, at four and a half miles per hour, melts off 440 calories per hour.

# SCANDINAVIAN SLALOMS

DURING MY TRIP to Norway, Lars leaped off his chair. "Let's go out," he said.

Horizontal on the couch, I put the magazine down and looked out the window. "Lars, it's snowing so hard, I can't even see the street," I replied.

Throwing a snowsuit at me, Lars just laughed. "Move it," he ordered playfully. Then a hat flew by my head, followed by plastic goggles.

"These boots should fit you and you can borrow my old skis," he said holding up a pair of battered boots. Initially, I resisted the idea, afraid I would look foolish.

"But I've never cross-country skied before," I stammered.

"Just try it," he insisted. "You have nothing to lose!"

Shaking my head, I shrugged and laughed. "Okay, let's go!"

Fumbling with my equipment, I finally got the skis on. Lars took the lead and shoved off. I teetered behind him, squinting between the snowflakes and trying to follow his movements by pushing out and back on the skis. I hobbled for the first few minutes trying to maintain my balance and then, suddenly found a rhythm. With poles balancing my movements, I was in the groove! We trekked through obscure paths and paved a few of our own. We arrived home three hours later, physically exhausted, but emotionally exhilarated. In the past, a snowy day meant I was confined to the house. Now I have a new winter option and can make the elements work for me!

> Dr. Jaap Seidell, Professor of Nutrition at the Free University of Amsterdam, believes that the much slower rate of weight gain in Holland, as well as in Sweden, Norway, and Denmark, is due to the enthusiastic, year-round participation by northern Europeans in all manner of outdoor activities, from soccer and hiking in the warmer months to cross-country skiing and ice skating in the winter. For example, cross-country skiing burns approximately 700 calories/hour.

# TOKYO TUBS

MY FRIEND DIANE and I had been talking about our trip to Tokyo for a month, but then she had to cancel the day of our intended departure because of a family emergency. When I hung up the phone, I sat down on the end of the bed. *"Now what?"* I thought to myself. Diane had planned the trip for us and now I knew little about our itinerary. Should I even go? Then I decided to view this solo opportunity as an adventure. I smiled to myself, *"Tokyo, here I come!"*

After a grueling fourteen-hour flight, then a restorative nap in my hotel room, I realized I was hungry. Leaving the hotel room for the Roppongi section of Tokyo, I looked above the mobs of pedestrians on the street and spotted a crowded, open-air eatery. Looking at the menu without knowing a single word of Japanese, I simply pointed at an item halfway down the page. The young waitress smiled at me and bowed. Smiling back at her and nodding my head in a simulated seated bow, I wondered how to say "pot luck" in Japanese. A few minutes later, the young lady and I again exchanged a series of nods and smiles as she placed a tray in front of me that contained a small bowl of soup, a plate of raw fish, and an egg. Having just woken up and not sure what time zone I was in, I went straight for what appeared to be the hard-boiled egg. "*A little breakfast before doing fish,*" I thought to myself. Tapping the egg on the tray to crack it, I was stunned to see egg whites started oozing onto my fingers. Not sure what to do, I simply dumped the raw egg into the soup. "*When in Tokyo . . . ,*" I thought, stirring the concoction with my chop sticks, picking up the bowl as I saw others in the restaurant do and downing the mixture. Next, I hungrily ate the fish. Feeling energized from the high-protein meal, I set out to explore.

The streets of Roppongi teemed with people and I was constantly elbow-to-elbow, whether I was on the street or in a store. The city was alive with neon signs flashing and a constant buzz of noise and activity. I returned to the hotel in serious need of some peace and relaxation. At the front desk, I spoke to Michi, a petite, soft-spoken college student with shiny black hair who was studying English. I asked Michi where locals went on vacation to escape the crowds.

"I take care," she said in her halting English. "You come here tomorrow morning."

The next morning, a driver was waiting for me in the hotel lobby. "You will relax," Michi promised, as we sped off.

The driver whisked me through the rolling green hills of the Japanese countryside and past a towering group of volcanoes on our way to a spa—one of almost two hundred in Japan. The volcanoes have created natural hot springs that are believed to ease arthritis and muscle joint pain. The car stopped in front of a small rustic-looking cabin and the driver nodded, motioning at the main door. He then pointed his finger to the number four on his watch and then pointed to the ground. I smiled and responded *"hai"* or "yes" with another nod, indicating that I understood our time to meet.

In exchange for a nominal fee, I received a towel and a key to a locker in the changing room. Quickly stripping and storing my clothes, I entered the pool area and was immediately assaulted by the smell of sulfur. Directly in front of me were five small pools, three of them filled with several dozing men and two completely empty. I went for the empty pool at the end and slipped in. Ouch! The bubbling water was burning hot. As the sweat streamed down my face, one of the local patrons motioned to me. "Vewy haht," he said, slowly pointing at my pool. "Leetle haht," he said as he motioned to the middle pool. "Not haht," he said as his arm swung toward the pool at the end.

*"Arrigato"* (thank you), I said, quickly clambering out of the boiling pool toward the least-hot pool.

"Ah, this is perfect," I said to myself as I immersed myself in its gentle warmth and I lollygagged the afternoon away in its thick, white waters, rubbing the natural minerals into my skin. My muscles, now limber from the heat, stretched easily, as I placed my hands under my feet and straightened my legs, and then clasped my hands above my head and arched backward to lengthen my back.

I returned back to Tokyo feeling revived and relaxed, my skin tingling and my body ready for a long night's sleep. The next day, I was more than ready for crowds and bustle again!

The American College of Sports Medicine (ACSM) has added recommendations for flexibility exercises to its most recent guidelines for adult fitness. ACSM experts advise stretching all major muscle groups a minimum of two to three days per week to stay limber and prevent injury.

# INDONESIAN INSIGHT

MARK, AN AMERICAN friend of mine, recently visited the Indonesian island of Bali. While relaxing at the quiet resort area of Nusa Dua, he noticed that at restaurants, the locals customarily sampled small portions of a variety of dishes on the table, in dramatic contrast to his American habit of ordering one large meal and scarfing up everything on his plate. When Mark went out with an Indonesian family, a generous bowl of rice, some bread, and several delicious appetizers were enjoyed by the entire table—and to Mark's surprise, he left the table satisfied.

"I loved the variety of tastes and eating communally," he told me. "It reminds me that I don't have to scrape my plate clean—and end up eating more than I really want."

Mark's experience resonated with me. Instead of finishing my meal just because it was in front of me, I started to check in with myself. Was I still hungry? If not, I stopped eating and asked the waiter to clear my plate from the table. When I go to restaurants known for large portions, to avoid temptation I now ask to take home half of it before the meal is served.

Jim Hart, nutritionist, personal trainer, and author of *Good to Go*, suggests that restaurant diners consider skipping the entrée entirely and instead ordering a large salad with an appetizer. Another idea: Enjoy a cup of soup, then split an entrée with your dinner companion.

# IRISH PIZZA

MARTHA, MARTIN, TRACY, and I were doing our best to enjoy Ireland. We'd rented a car in Dublin and were trying to drive on the left side of the road. We picked straws and Martin lost. As he opened the door on the right side of the car and slid behind the wheel, he laughed. "It will be strange seated on this side."

Because we'd opted for the most economical car, it had a standard shift that we had to operate with the left hand. The gears made a grinding noise in rebellion and the car bucked and stalled repeatedly.

"We'll be lucky if we get home in one piece," Martha shrieked as a car sped by our right side going in the opposite direction.

Finally, we got the hang of left-handed shifting, took turns driving, and spent several enjoyable days touring the picturesque countryside, walking through the tiny towns and eating in local pubs. By then, we were ready for a more urban experience.

"Let's check out Belfast," Tracy said.

In Belfast, we walked through Donegal Square, past City Hall and lounged lazily on the grass in the quaint courtyard near Queen's University. Hungry, we started looking for a lunch spot and the first one we saw was Pizza Hut.

"Pizza works for me," Tracy said.

"I don't typically eat fast food," Martha added, "but after all the heavy local fare, a personal pan pizza sounds good to me."

I ordered a personal pan pizza and looked forward to stuffing myself with some "down home" American food. Flipping open the top of the container, I found a *very* small pizza, the size of a large doughnut. Disappointed, I ordered a small salad to go with it. To my surprise, after finishing this smaller (and healthier) meal, I found myself sated and content. I also found myself wondering: *Are most "American-style" portions supersized—and are we paying a price for it?*

According to Psychologist Paul Rozin, Pizza Hut personal pan pizzas in Europe are approximately two-thirds the size of personal pan pizzas in the United States. According to an article in the August 14, 2004, *Wall Street Journal,* a serving of Philadelphia Cream Cheese marketed to U.S. consumers contains fourteen percent more calories than the same size serving in Italy. A jar of Hellmann's Mayonnaise purchased in the United Kingdom has half the saturated fat of the Hellmann's sold in the United States. Kellogg's All-Bran bought in the United States has three times the sodium as the same brand sold in Mexico. A standard beverage bottle for sodas in Europe is about half a pint—roughly half the amount of the standard sixteen-ounce can sold in the United States. Perhaps it's no wonder that the United States has the highest rate of obesity in the world.

# EGYPTIAN INGENUITY

RIMA IS A dark-eyed thirty-five-year-old Egyptian mother of three teenage boys who lives in the upper-middle class suburb of Mahdi, just outside Cairo. The area, home to the American School of Cairo, boasts many large well-kept homes. The upscale area is inhabited mainly by foreigners, with lush green yards constantly barraged by sprinklers to keep the ground damp in the intense heat.

Rima and her husband, Khalil met at Stanford University on a blind date, married and returned to Egypt after the birth of their first son. "Although I'm a mechanical engineer, my family is my priority," Rima told me during a visit to their home. Her sultry brown eyes are set off by thick black hair pulled back with a clip. She has struggled in her efforts to balance family, job, and other responsibilities.

"This is what happened when I went back to work," Rima said holding up a picture with a chuckle. I looked at a family portrait of Rima, Khalil, and their three sons, all recognizable but noticeably heavier!

"It seems like a lifetime ago," Rima murmured as she shook her head, "but it's only been a year." In the interim, Rima lost fifty pounds, her husband sixty pounds, and her sons more than twenty pounds each.

"Two years ago, when I returned to work, we began to eat on the go," said Rima. "Fast food became a way of life. I knew I had to do something."

After some thought, Rima put a new plan into effect. She devised a long list of possible meals, all heavily reliant on the fresh vegetables that typify traditional Egyptian fare. On each Saturday morning, the family scans the list and decides as a group what their meals will be for the week. Rima shops that afternoon accordingly.

Then, on Sundays, the fun begins. Each family member picks a day that he or she is responsible for. Then, as a team, they assemble their meals together. The only snacks Rima allows in the house are fresh fruits and vegetables, with a few exceptions.

"Once a month, I bring home something sweet as a treat and we enjoy it as a family," Rima says with a smile. "But I always keep the fruit bowl well stocked and sliced carrots and celery in the fridge."

Khalil has enjoyed the change. "Not only are we healthier, but the ritual is fun and a chance for us to spend time together, bonding and making decisions as a family team," he says. "Inevitably, somebody ends up covered in flour or forgets part of the recipe," he chuckles, "but we have a lot of laughs along the way!"

Most importantly, Rima and Khalil know that their family is eating delicious, well-balanced meals.

One of the family's favorite meals is stuffed *koosa* (squash or zucchini). While traditionally *koosa* is filled with ground beef, Rima has devised a tasty vegetarian alternative.

**Vegetarian Stuffed *Koosa***

10 medium squash or zucchini
Pam spray
3/4 cup minced onion
1/2 pound of fresh diced seasonal vegetables
1/4 cup pine nuts
1 teaspoon salt
1/2 teaspoon pepper
1 1/2 cups tomato juice or diluted tomato paste
1 cup water

1. Preheat oven to 350° F.
2. Wash the squash/zucchini well and trim the ends.
3. Sauté in a frying pan coated with Pam spray and then drain into shallow baking pan or Pyrex dish.
4. Sauté onion in same frying pan coated with Pam until soft. Add diced vegetables, pine nuts, salt, and pepper and sauté until vegetables are *al dente.*
5. Slice each squash/zucchini lengthwise and remove some of the seeds.

6. Fill the pocket with the vegetable mixture, cover with tomato juice or paste, and sprinkle with salt and pepper.
7. Bake for 20 minutes to brown the tops and then serve. (Hint: This dish freezes well for future use.)

In December 2002, the U.S. Surgeon General declared obesity a bona-fide epidemic. And it isn't just adults who are out of shape. According to Dr. Ellen S. Bass, a pediatric specialist, forty percent of American children are overweight and almost fifteen percent are obese. If this trend continues, says Baylor University weight-loss researcher Dr. John Foreyt, in just twenty-five years nearly every American will be dangerously overweight.

# POLISH PASSIONS

A EUROPEAN FRIEND once said to me, "If you love Vienna and Prague, you will love Krakow," and she was right. As I sat in Old Town Square, in the heart of Poland's most charming city, I watched horses and carriages parade by on traditional cobblestoned streets with ornate, medieval buildings as a backdrop. I felt as though I were watching a movie—or better yet, was in the middle of one. I walked up a small hill and entered St. Mary's church and discovered a breathtaking interior with intricate stained glass and a dark blue ceiling sparkling with stars. The church overlooked the square, offering onlookers an unparalleled view of the center of town, with its upscale restaurants and sassy jazz clubs.

Early in the evening, I met Karel, a tall, athletic blond woman with tumbling curls pulled back in a ponytail. A friend of a friend, she met me for dinner at a restaurant on the square where we enjoyed dumpling soup and "*golabki,*" cabbage rolls filled with chicken. Karel's face was flushed and her cheeks glowed as she told me about her recent hiking trip through the Tatra Mountains just outside Krakow. "Tomorrow I am going ice skating," she revealed.

The next day I intended to go sightseeing, but I was exhausted from jet lag. Halfway through the day, I threw in the towel and went back to my hotel. After a short nap, I watched television for the remainder of the afternoon. Realizing the day was slipping away, I leaped out of bed and prepared to meet Karel for dinner.

At dinner, Karel detailed another active day. She jogged in the morning, met a friend for lunch, and went food shopping in the afternoon.

"Don't you *ever* lie around and read or watch television?" I asked guiltily.

"No," she laughed. "Television is boring and I feel better if I keep moving."

Two weeks later, back in the United States, I *thought* I was exhausted. I found myself at home lying on the couch watching television. Then I thought of Karel, got up and forced myself to go for a bike ride. Halfway through the ride, I could feel my body begin to purr with delight. I returned home rejuvenated and energized.

> According to a study by time researcher John P. Robinson from the University of Maryland, Americans watch more television than any other population in the world— tuning in fifty percent more than the French and Germans do, and fully twice as much as the Poles and Hungarians. Over the last twenty years, American time in front of the TV has crept up by an average of five hours per week—a disturbing thirty percent increase.

# PORTUGUESE PERSPECTIVE

ALTHOUGH MY TRIP to visit my friend Juan in Portugal had been planned for months, I wasn't sure if I should go. Two days before my scheduled departure, Chris, a dear friend in the United States, called to tell me he had cancer and was preparing for chemotherapy. After several phone calls and reassurances from Chris's wife that I should keep my travel plans, I guiltily decided to leave.

After an uneventful flight, Juan picked me up at the airport and we drove to Juan's apartment. After I showered, we drove to the ancient Castle of Saint George outside Lisbon. As we approached the landmark, I saw geese and ducks parading through the manicured gardens and a dry moat surrounding the massive, gray-stoned fortress. Yet somehow, I couldn't focus on the beauty around me. Juan and I climbed up the tower on top and I found myself sitting on a ledge overlooking the magnificent landscape.

"Are you okay?" Juan asked. "You seem so quiet."

Nibbling on my thumbnail, I told Juan about my concern for Chris. I talked about our close friendship in college and how honored I was to be an usher in his wedding.

"An old friend," I said quietly. "The type of friend you don't see everyday, but when you get together, it seems like you were never apart."

Juan nodded. "Come on," he said patting me lightly on the back. "Let's get something to eat, then we'll head back to my place where you can relax," he said.

After entering the restaurant, we were seated in the center of the main floor, surrounded by talkative diners and the characteristic "jush" sound of the Portuguese language. The waiter handed us menus, but I couldn't concentrate on the offerings.

"Can you order for us?" I asked. "Whatever you are having works for me." He nodded and we sat silently. I felt empty and exhausted.

When our meals arrived, I all but attacked my plate. After a few short moments, I had finished my entrée, potatoes, and string beans. The only particles remaining on my plate were some fish bones. Looking up, I saw the horror on Juan's face. He hadn't yet taken a bite. Looking at the diners next to us, I realized they'd received their food before us, yet their plates had hardly been touched. I saw the man at the table next to us cut a small piece of steak, slowly put the tiny serving in his mouth, then rest his utensils on his plate as he talked to his companion. Then he took a sip of wine and continued conversing. Every few minutes he would repeat this ritual.

"Bill, why did you eat so fast?" Juan whispered.

"I . . . I don't know," I responded. "I'm just out of sorts." Fidgeting in my seat, I stared at Juan while he slowly consumed his meal.

"I want ice cream," I said suddenly. Before Juan could respond, I motioned for the waiter. "Ice cream, please," I said. "Large, any flavor."

That evening I thought about the way I'd wolfed down my dinner. I wondered why I was so out of control. Maybe food was my coping mechanism under stress, I thought. Or perhaps, because the Portuguese use their meals as a chance to reconnect with friends and family, they're less likely to overeat in the way we often do—using food *itself* as a substitute source of comfort and connection. *"Probably a combination of the two,"* I thought to myself.

The next day, after a solid night's rest, I felt better. I was adjusting to the idea of Chris having cancer, and I began to focus positive thoughts and energy on a healthy recovery. Making a conscious effort to eat more slowly, I enjoyed my lunch the next day and matched Juan's relaxed pace. I tasted, and savored, every bite.

According to John P. Robinson, author of *Time for Life,* the Portuguese spend twenty percent more time eating than Americans do, yet they are less likely to be overweight than we are. In addition, according to an article in the April 3, 2003, *Wall Street Journal,* many Americans deal with stress, loneliness, and life's uncertainties by eating excess amounts of unhealthy food. During the first Gulf War, and immediately after the 2001 terrorist attacks, Americans ate more take-out and consumed substantially more fat and calories than during peace times. Example: Rouge, an upscale bistro in Philadelphia, sold 560 hamburgers in the first week of the 2003 Iraqi conflict—nearly twice the usual number.

# 5
# This Thing Called LOVE

# SOUTH AFRICAN SYNERGY

TRACY AND I were mesmerized by the beauty of Capetown, especially Table Mountain, which naturally encases and nuzzles the downtown area, with magnificent gardens at the base of the mountain that shimmy down to the sea. A short drive outside the city takes you past vast vineyards and leafy wildlife preserves. It is one of the most naturally charming spots in the world.

One evening, to celebrate Tracy's birthday, we chose one of the fanciest restaurants in Capetown, where we dined sitting on a stately marble balcony overlooking the beach below. The sounds of the tides lapping the shore, the subtle lanterns lighting up the swaying trees in front of us, and the soft candlelight created a dreamlike, magical ambiance. Seated at the table next to us were Madeline and Frank, an attractive and jovial couple in their sixties. Madeline had short, spiky silver hair that matched her shiny silver beaded dress and long dangling earrings, setting off her sun-kissed face. Frank, her husband, wore a bright smile and a snappy, three-button navy suit with a yellow bow tie. We couldn't help noticing this couple because they were obviously having so much fun—they laughed throughout dinner while holding hands across the table. As Frank animatedly told stories—flapping his arms and tilting his head as he spoke—Madeline hooted and slapped her thigh. She repeatedly pleaded, "stop, stop!" waving her hands as she wiped the tears away.

"You two are the best," I said to them. Madeline explained that they were celebrating their fortieth wedding anniversary.

"That's great," Tracy exclaimed. "What's your secret?"

Madeline didn't miss a beat. "You have to marry your best friend," she said as she squeezed Frank's hand and winked at him. "And make sure your best friend has a sense of humor!"

> In the April 29, 2003, issue of *Psychology Today,* psychologist Hara Marano writes "of all the elements that contribute to the warm atmosphere of a good relationship, there is one . . . that everyone desires and most would like more of—laughter."

# SAIGON NUPTIALS

A FLIGHT ATTENDANT friend, Regine, a tall, slim African American woman, had always been fascinated with Vietnam. Her father told her amazing stories about falling in love with a Vietnamese girl during the war. Through his girlfriend, her father was able to experience the gentle side of Vietnamese life and culture during a politically contentious time. Now, thirty years later, Regine and her new husband, Thomas, were walking the humid streets of Saigon, which buzzed with the clatter of small shops, the clicking of motorcycle gears, and the chatter of passersby.

As Regine and Thomas wound their way through the residential streets outside Saigon, they saw a crowd of beaming faces coming toward them. The group was an eclectic mix—couples strolling arm-in-arm, children skipping, singles jogging. Regine saw an older woman at the back of the group, waving her cane and smiling from ear-to-ear as she tried to keep up with the pack.

Regine grabbed Thomas by the arm and said, "Let's join the party."

They hovered in the back of the crowd as a young tuxedo-clad man led the group from door to door, gathering neighbors and friends at each stop. As the group grew, the sounds of laughter, chatter, and celebratory whooping escalated to a feverish pitch. Regine smiled at an older man standing next to her.

"It's a wedding," he whispered in English, bringing the index fingers of both hands together. Then, as the group clustered around a particular doorway, they fell silent. The door opened, revealing a beaming bride with a long white dress and matching shoulder-length veil. People lined up in front of the door, presenting the bride with gifts of money.

The older man's daughter, who spoke impeccable English, joined her father at the back of the line and told Regine about the Vietnamese approach to marriage.

"All the friends and family present the bride with cash to start the couple on their way in life," she explained. "The only person who doesn't join the party is the groom's mother, to show the bride there is no rivalry between the two women for the groom's attention."

As the crowd moved along, Regine and Thomas stayed back, not wanting to intrude. Regine reflected on her own wedding and how much debt she and her husband had incurred for their gala. She also thought about the number of gifts they received that didn't meet their needs or their lifestyle.

"Gifts of money might have been more helpful to us," she mused to Thomas.

"Yes," he said wryly, "we're still paying for that day. Maybe we could have bought a house by now."

"And I *really* like the part about the mother-in-law taking a backseat," Regine added, with a playful poke into her husband's ribs. Thomas laughed and hugged her.

"You know you're number one," he said.

"Yeah, I just wish *she* knew that!" Regine exclaimed, returning her husband's embrace.

According to a Bank of America survey of 1,200 American brides and grooms, more than seventy percent will spend at least $10,000 to say "I do." Of those, more than a quarter will spend $20,000 or more. Fully sixty-eight percent of engaged couples expect to go over budget—and many will spend several years paying off their debt.

# LOVE IN THE ANDES?

DIMITRA WAS ON the phone. "Hey, want to go hiking in Ecuador next month?" she asked.

"Why," I asked. "What's there?"

Dimitra responded, "I've found this eco-lodge in Cotopaxi, right in the heart of the Andes. It looks great!"

I went straight to the Internet and looked it up. I called Dimitra right back. "Count me in," I enthused and we both whooped.

After an uneventful flight to Quito and a harrowing three-hour drive on dusty, pebbled roads, we arrived at our lodge. On the second day, we signed up for an adventure. Halfway through a ten-mile hike, scaling the Andes, I thought I was going to collapse and wondered what had made me think this would be a fun challenge. Gasping for breath at the 11,000-foot elevation, I looked down at the clouds. But I persevered, eventually climbing into and around Crater Lake, the dormant volcano that surrounds a crystal blue lake in the heart of the Andes. Huffing and puffing, Dimitra and I lagged behind the other ten members of the group, an eclectic mix of twenty-something European couples—including Scots, Brits, Irish, Swedes, and Italians.

Along the way, our hiking group bonded, helping each other up steep climbs over jagged cliffs and traipsing through narrow, dusty ravines. We shared water, food, and words of support. Still at the back of the pack, I was especially appreciative of the kind words of encouragement for Dimitra and me—the "senior members," who were almost two decades older than the rest of the group. Upon returning to our rustic lodge, we gathered around the large, oak table for a family-style dinner. I purposely sat down at the center of the table, knowing I wanted to get to know these people better.

As we feasted on delicious vegetarian fare, I asked with a chuckle, "So, are you all married or traveling in sin?"

Angela, a slim, attractive British woman with shiny black hair responded, "Well, we might get married, depending on how the rest of the trip goes."

Her boyfriend Chris laughed. "So far, so good," he said.

"That depends if Chris starts cleaning up after himself," Angela retorted. Chris smirked. Angela and Chris went on to say that they had dated for two years and after saving money for the last year, quit their jobs and decided to tour South America together for three months.

"Chris used to keep his flat in Bristol quite tidy," Angela added. "Evidently, he was on his best behavior at home because now he's quite sloppy—and I'm *not* going to pick up after him." It was obvious Angela and Chris had hit a snag in their relationship and like most couples, were trying to figure out their roles, identify expectations, and negotiate a way of being together they both could live with.

"You're all quite gutsy," I remarked, "traveling together halfway around the world to the Andes."

"No, not really, it's quite common." piped in Marie, a former secretary from Sweden. "Bjorn and I are doing the same thing."

Andrea, an Italian woman from Bologna nodded. "So are we," she said, motioning toward her partner Gianni. The other couples around the table nodded in agreement.

I must have looked stunned because Andrea, an assertive, athletic psychotherapist who had studied in the United States, added with a grin, "I know this is hard to understand for many Americans. You see, this trip is a chance for us to see if we are compatible in the long-term. We're together twenty-four hours a day, seven days a week, for several months. We venture to strange lands together and find our way through obstacles like language difficulties, getting sick from strange food, riding on the wrong buses, or just plain getting lost."

The others in the group smiled and nodded. "It's an analogy for life together as a couple," concluded Andrea. "We find out lots about each other—who takes the lead and how easy are they to get along with." She put her arm around her boyfriend and kissed him on the cheek. "Last month I knew Gianni was the one for me. I fell down a ravine and sprained my ankle. Gianni remained calm and got me medical assistance," she said, stroking his cheek. "I knew I could count on him in a crisis. But just as importantly, we've found out that we can have fun with each other."

Gianni, a car mechanic from Bologna, good-naturedly threw up his hands and added "And you can see who is boss here!" As the group roared with laughter, I felt the connection between us solidify.

Everyone had contributed to the conversation except the Scottish couple seated quietly at the end of the table. Kathleen and Philip are both twenty-four years old. As I looked at them expectantly, the rest of the table followed my gaze.

Kathleen haltingly began, "Philip isn't quite . . . quite as strong as I thought he might be." Philip's lips tightened.

"I don't speak the bloody language and you can't expect me to do everything," he snapped. Kathleen stared into her lap. Philip grimaced and his right foot tapped repeatedly on the floor. In the long lull that followed, the only sound that could be heard was a chair scraping along the floor as someone uncomfortably twitched.

Andrea broke the uncomfortable silence. "Eet takes a woman to be a leader!" she declared and the group broke into nervous laughter. Adding to the humor, Gianni threw his hands up again in mock despair and the group laughed again—this time joined even by Kathleen and Philip. Then, the door of the lodge opened and two other couples—one from Belgium, the other from Spain—shuffled their bags into the dining area. As we greeted them, I wondered, *"If American couples spent more time together—especially on 'twenty-four seven' vacations with each other—would many of us make different partner choices?"*

> According to *Divorce Magazine,* the United States has the highest divorce rate of any major country in the world. The probability of a newly married American couple sustaining a long-term marriage is only forty-one percent.

# JAPANESE SOLOS

AT MIDNIGHT ON my third day in Tokyo, I was still jet-lagged, wide awake, and staring at the ceiling of my hotel room. Clambering out of bed, I got dressed and made my way to the lobby. Fortunately, the lounge was still open and a hostess quickly sat me at a table next to three well-dressed Japanese women in their thirties. I nodded, smiled, and said "good evening" in English as I passed their table. The three nodded and silently covered their smiles with their hands. When I sent each of them a drink, I was rewarded with a cacophony of giggles. But when I opened my hands, gesturing to them to join me, two of the women bowed and left the lounge. The third woman, however, shyly joined my table.

"Bill," I said extending my hand.

"Mitsuko," she responded, with her eyes cast downward and her long black hair hiding her face. In the awkward moment that followed, I explained I only wanted to get to know more about the Japanese culture for a book I was writing.

"A book!" she said. "I want to be in a book."

As Mitsuko coiled her long hair behind her ears, illuminating her long, thin porcelain face, I asked her about her life. She told me she was an executive secretary with an American firm, which explained her excellent English. When I asked about relationships, her face softened.

"No husband, no children," at which point she smiled, "no problems," she declared. She sat back in her chair with a big smile.

Mitsuko told me that many modern Japanese women don't want the responsibility of being a wife or mother. "It's too much," she explained. "Traditional Japanese women take care of everybody with no energy for themselves."

I thought about a number of cultures where women are often overwhelmed. I wondered: *Are Japanese women's priorities changing or is Mitsuko's experience part of a regional or global trend?*

According to the Japanese Ministry of Public Management, fifty-four percent of Japanese women between the ages of twenty-five and twenty-nine were unmarried in 2000—three times the rate of unmarried Japanese women in the same age group in 1970. In addition, about half of single Japanese women ages thirty-five to fifty-four have no intention of marrying, according to a survey by the Japan Institute of Life Insurance.

# DUTCH DUOS

I MET GRETA and Werner, her boyfriend, at a party in The Hague. Both previously married, they were looking for ways to intensify their relationship as a couple without actually living together.

Each of them, they told me, enjoyed their own homes, furnished to their own tastes. Greta liked her contemporary furnishings that reflected clean, simple lines. Werner, by contrast, collected antiques and decorated his home with wall-to-wall knick-knacks. I wondered: Is that really *all* that's keeping them apart? Later, over dinner, they filled me in.

"I have to have a spotless house with no clutter," Greta emphatically stated. Then her face softened. "On the other hand, I respect the way Werner lives and his right to do so. But it just would not work for me."

Werner laughed. "Okay, I can be sloppy, but I enjoy a comfortable, lived-in atmosphere. Greta's house is nice, but it's not soothing to me."

There were additional complications. Werner smoked cigars and Greta detested smoke in her house.

Werner shrugged, "It's my house and I want to feel comfortable smoking in it.

Chimed in Greta, "I am hoping he will quit, but I also realize that I can't change him. He has to make his own decisions."

Werner nodded, "That's right," he said. "You knew I smoked when you met me and you accepted it. I am content the way I am."

In addition, Greta had three children in their early twenties from her previous marriage.

"Werner has no children and I don't want him to feel he has inherited mine," she explained.

"Of course my kids are on their own, but I want them to know they have a welcoming place to come and live if they hit a snag in life." Werner clarified, "I like her kids and they are always welcome in my home on holidays or for visits. But I just don't know if I want them living with me."

Neither one wanted to merge finances. "It isn't that I don't want to share with Greta, because I do. However, we have to look at the realities in life and realize that we may not work out in the long run," Werner said.

Greta added, "Werner is very generous. But I don't want him to think I'm with him because he has more than I do."

For many months, Greta and Werner discussed their choices. "We talked about several conventional options—to continue dating, to live together, or even to get married," Greta disclosed.

Werner chimed in, "But we both knew that we simply had very different ways of living and any one of those differences could be a recipe for disaster."

Greta added, "And as you can see, there are just a *few* differences!" Both threw their heads back and laughed. Greta concluded, "Yet we knew we wanted to be together."

Werner reached out to hold Greta's hand as they emphatically nodded their agreement.

Their solution? They bought a duplex outside Amsterdam and split the purchase price so that they could live side by side—right next door to each other while maintaining their own space. They maintain a small cache of clothing and toiletries at each other's home so they can stay over at a moment's notice.

"It's really ideal for us," Greta said. "I have my things around me, and the house is spotless."

"And smokeless," Werner added, giving Greta a poke in the ribs. "It's a perfect solution for us," Werner added. "We are both happy and relaxed. It's nice to retain our independence, yet still be a couple."

| |
|---|
| Love always finds a way. |

# OVER-THE-TOP ROMAN ROMANCE

ON A TRIP to Rome, I met Gabriella, a cousin of a close family friend. She is slim and fashionable, wearing spiked heels that make her appear much taller than five feet. Her jet-black hair is cut in a stylish, layered bob that frames her face and large brown eyes. Renaldo, her husband of eleven years, can't take his eyes off her. As they sit close together on the couch, they are constantly in contact—Gabriella gently twirling the hairs on Renaldo's forearms or Renaldo lightly caressing her back.

"Sometimes it doesn't seem possible, but things just get better and better between us," Gabriella said, nuzzling Renaldo. "I think time keeps bringing our relationship to new levels of trust and respect. The key for me is to let Renaldo know how much I adore him."

Renaldo jumped in with "We are Italian and we love life," as his hands flailed in the air. "I married the *bella* Gabriella," he continued, his eyes filling, "and I thought the day we married was the best day of my life. But my time with her just keeps getting better." He wipes away a tear as he said, "I am such a lucky man."

Renaldo had more to tell me. "One day I was thinking, 'I

love this woman so much. I want to be with her right now, but I want it to be special.' So, I went to Gabriella's job and kidnapped her."

Gabriella threw her head back and shrieked with laughter. Renaldo recalled how he had walked into her office, went behind her desk, pulled out a handkerchief, and blindfolded her. Then he took her hand and led her outside to his car while her coworkers clapped and cheered.

Gabriella threw her arms around Renaldo's shoulders and rocked him. "It was wonderful. I didn't know where I was or where we were going till I recognized the sounds of a train station and heard the boarding announcement for the bullet train to Venice."

"We had a wonderful time," Gabriella said wistfully as she put her hand on Renaldo's thigh.

"We had our own cabin on the train and we had a really incredible ride to Venice," he added, squeezing her hand. Gabriella squeezed back and said, *"Si, si bello."*

I wondered: *Does the key to maintaining a long-term, loving relationship lie in keeping the dramatic romance and element of surprise alive?*

> *Divorce Magazine* reports that Italy has the lowest divorce rate in Europe and one of the lowest divorce rates in the world.

# FLY AWAY

LAURA AND I met at a party in New York. She is an outspoken, intelligent forty-two-year-old American who landed an incredible job as a lead dispatcher with the national airline in Thailand. While working in Bangkok, she met a Thai man, Tam, and the two began a courtship. They escaped to the resort area of Chang Mai for long romantic weekends, complete with sunset walks through Khao Sok National Park and slow, lumbering elephant rides through the countryside.

"Tam was polite, gracious, and warm," Laura told me. "We were together for over a year and I think he was intrigued by my confidence and capabilities, but on the other hand he probably thought I was too aggressive." Her face softened and she ran her index finger over her lip. "I knew in the long run we probably weren't going to work," she mused. "We come from such different worlds. He never wanted to leave Thailand. I loved living there but I couldn't imagine staying forever. The line was drawn in the sand. Anyway, I knew I had to break it off, but I didn't know how."

Laura went to Chang Mai for a few days to figure out how to break the relationship off. She went into a local monastery and sat in silence, praying for guidance. Having no luck, she made her way toward a small restaurant across the street, where she planned to order jasmine tea. Next to the restaurant, she saw a tiny store with a number of cages out front, each cage filled with a single bird. The man waved at Laura and motioned toward himself.

"Come," he invited. Laura smiled and crossed the road. "Lady, you tell bird problems, then let it fly away. Problems go, too."

"I'll take that bird," Laura said without hesitation, pointing to a blue and green feathered bird closest to her. "At that point," she laughs, "I was willing to do anything." She walked with her new bird and cage to the top of the hill surrounding the town, where she found a small patch of grass on which to sit with her new pet.

"I told that bird everything," Laura said, "from the time I met Tam right up to that day." Then she simply sat and cried. When she stopped crying, she opened the cage and watched the bird fly away.

"I don't know if the old custom really worked or if it was just the opportunity to talk it through from start to finish," said Laura. "But I felt much better afterward and I returned to Bangkok with little sadness and a solid plan I didn't have before."

Love is like a bird. Set it free. If it comes back, it is yours. If it doesn't, it never was.

# VICTORIAN WEDDING

I MET KEITH at his sister's barbecue in Chicago. He is an architect and an avid cyclist from Vancouver. The day after the get-together, we cycled around the city and along Lake Michigan.

"You always have a place to stay in Vancouver," Keith said.

"I've always wanted to go there," I replied. "You'll see me next month!"

I was impressed by Vancouver, a modern city, with clean-lined high-rises and office buildings that seem to slope into the Pacific Ocean, akin to its charming sister city, Seattle.

"Are you up for a quick trip to Victoria?" Keith asked. "My neighbor is getting married tomorrow on the island and I can bring a guest."

I flashed on my sparsely packed carry-on. "I'd love to go to Victoria, but I didn't bring a suit for a wedding," I replied.

"Actually, you're fine in khakis and a button down," he assured me. "They are getting married on the beach at sunset." The next morning we boarded the boat for the short ride to Victoria.

As the boat pulled into the harbor, I felt as though I'd been transported to the English countryside as I admired quaint lanes and small cottages along tree-lined streets. In the enchanting downtown area, I could see castles that turned out to be government buildings. Adding to the charm, a temperate weather system surrounds the island, virtually guaranteeing that everyday will be sunny and moderate, with temperatures rarely dipping below forty degrees or surging above eighty degrees.

Keith drove as I read the simple directions. "Must be over there," I said as I spotted a group of about twenty cars.

Keith pulled up, hopped out of the car, slipped off his shoes, rolled up his slacks, and bolted for the beach. "Let's go!"

I followed Keith, ambling through the sand toward the small crowd. The sun was setting and the sky was aglow with purple and orange hues. The wind seemed to pick up the closer we got to the water, just in time to see two white veils flying in the air.

"Lesbians?" I whispered to Keith. "I have never been to a lesbian wedding before." Actually, there was nothing different about this wedding. It was a very touching and loving, with the couple glowing as they exchanged vows and rings. The parents smiled with joy and hugged all the guests. At the reception on the beach, we sipped champagne and feasted on fresh salmon.

"I guess I should have told you before it was two women," Keith laughed as we drove back to the dock for the last boat to Vancouver, "But it's just not a big deal here in Canada. What two adults do is between them and if two people can find love together, that is great."

According to the International Gay and Lesbian Human Rights Commission, Canada, Holland, and Belgium recognize gay marriage. Additionally, Sweden, Luxembourg, Spain, and Switzerland recognize gay civil partnerships and are considering recognizing gay marriage.

# 6
# Embracing Your SEXUALITY

# SAUNA SHENANIGANS

SEVERAL WINTERS AGO I found myself on a layover in Wiesbaden, Germany, a picturesque suburb just outside of Frankfurt. The hotel had a number of nice amenities, including a decent workout area with a small lap pool and dry sauna. *Perfect,* I thought. After an invigorating dip in the pool, I made my way to the sauna for some much anticipated solitude. Before long, two parents and their teenage son and daughter entered the sauna. As I watched, they chattered and laughed, all the while casually peeling off their bathing suits. Panic-stricken and confused, I all but ran out of the room. Later, once I'd recovered my equilibrium, I chalked up the scene to the antics of one bizarre family. *What could they have been thinking?*

As if I were destined to learn a cultural lesson, I found myself in Copenhagen the following summer. After a full day of touring, cruising through the surrounding canals by boat, and briskly strolling through Tivoli Gardens, I made my way to the hotel gym. After a session on the Stairmaster and a couple of sets on the universal weights, I went to the spa area to meditate and relax. Opening the door to the steam room, I was accosted by a wave of thick, hot steam and several voices conversing animatedly. After a few minutes, my body adjusted to the escalated heat of the room and I relaxed and looked around.

To my left were four businessmen, all in their late forties, chatting about the convention they had attended earlier that day. Directly across from me was a group of three women and two men in their late twenties, telling jokes and laughing loudly (and who, I found out later, had just met in the steam room). On my right was a family—two thirty-something parents and three children ranging in age from six to twelve. Except for me, everyone in the room was completely naked.

I had been raised in a number of countries and was comfortable with many cultural practices, but when it came to public displays of nudity, I was all-American. In my family, we always carefully covered our bodies. I felt my shoulders rise to my ears as I stared miserably at the teak floor board under my feet, subconsciously holding my hands over my crotch.

As I stood to leave, the woman across the way called out to me in English, "You're American, aren't you?"

Looking up, I saw that she was fully exposed, with one leg hiked up and her hands clasped around her knee, which only partially hid her large breasts.

Looking quickly away, I mumbled "Yes . . . how did you know?"

Laughing, she responded, "Americans are *so* uncomfortable with their bodies!"

The following winter, as I vacationed on the Caribbean island of Saint Martin, I was determined to more fully understand my experience. I had read about Orient Beach, often described as one of the most beautiful stretches of beach in the world, and which has a "clothing-optional" section frequented by tourists from around the world. I decided to visit the beach, talk to nudists, and try to gain a better understanding of their approach to their bodies. Orient Beach is cut in two by a small jutting hill of milky white sand.

"How does this place work?" I asked a local shopkeeper.

"Bathing suits to the left, nudists to the right," he placidly responded, gazing out at the azure sea.

I asked him where most Americans went and where most Europeans went. Now he smiled broadly as he replied "Americans to the left, Europeans to the right," nodding in each direction.

With a sigh of trepidation, I began my journey to the right. If I was going to interview nudists with any credibility, I knew I would have to shed my own shorts. Halfway down the beach, I took a big gulp of air, reached down, and pulled my shorts down and off. Looking up, I thought with horror *"What if I get . . . excited?"* I decided I would immediately sprint for the cool ocean. But ironically, it wasn't a sexually charged atmosphere; the hundreds of international visitors appeared to be very relaxed and simply enjoying a sunny day at the beach. Within a few minutes, my anxiety dissipated. With the exception of my sunglasses, I was wearing nothing. I felt warm all over and very free.

Overhearing an older couple chatting in French, I decided this was my opportunity. I introduced myself in French and explained that I was an American doing some research on international ways of living. This got the attention of a nearby German couple and two Spanish girls traveling together, and they joined our conversation.

Jacques, the French husband, began: "Here on this beach, it doesn't matter if you're the President of France or a street vendor," he declared. "We are all the same and it is very liberating. There is nothing to hide behind."

Genevieve, his wife added, "Although we are naked, we're not necessarily feeling sexual. One needs more than just the physical to become aroused."

"But at the same time," one of the Spanish girls said playfully, "feeling good about your body makes sex better!"

We all laughed, but then the German man brought the conversation back to a more serious plane.

"It's really about being authentic," he observed. He poked his ample belly and then affectionately stroked his wife's plump thigh. "We're not perfect, but we are happy with ourselves. Look around. Most people are not perfect-looking and when you see that, you can find peace with yourself."

At that moment, I realized that I was naked in front of strangers and I didn't care. Suddenly, I felt a bit more accepting of my own body. It wasn't perfect; it wasn't flawed. It was simply me.

According to *Newsweek*, an estimated twenty percent of married couples in the United States report a reluctance to undress in front of their spouses.

# YOU SEXY THING

MARTA IS AN attractive thirty-eight-year-old marketing executive who lives in Barcelona with Enrico, her forty-three-year-old boyfriend. Marta loves to dress seductively for work and acknowledges appreciative glances with a smile. In fact, she occasionally walks by a construction site and waves and blows kisses to all "the boys" while they hoot and holler. When she told me this, my American sensibilities were shocked. I asked her if her actions didn't invite unsolicited requests or trouble.

She responded, "I am a big girl. I have only had one direct confrontation when I had to look someone in the eye and forcefully tell him I am involved with someone. But then I smiled and told him I appreciated his remarks," she added with a wink. The point: All of this flirtation makes Marta feel *very* sexy. "I return at the end of the day sexually charged and I can't get enough," she laughs. "In fact, sometimes I think I am wearing Enrico out!"

Certainly, Marta's behavior could invite troublesome reactions in some parts of the world. However, her key point—the importance of inhabiting our sexuality—is well taken. As Americans, many of us adopt a dizzying number of daily personas, from competent business people to doting parents to home-maintenance experts to responsible shoppers and innovative chefs, all within a twenty-four-hour period. At the end of an exhausting day, passionate lover may be just one personality transition too many. Marta doesn't have to make that "persona" shift because she has made the sexual side of her an integral part of her being.

A 2004 poll of more than 16,000 Americans surveyed by *Men's Fitness* and *Shape* magazines found that both men and women avoid sexual situations because they're uncomfortable with their bodies—nearly fifty percent of women and twenty-four percent of men.

# TURN THE TABLES

SOMETIMES EXCITING SEX is ignited by some gender-bending role reversals—and a dash of fun. Dimitri is a burly forty-five-year-old banker who lives on the Greek side of the Mediterranean island of Cyprus. After fifteen years of marriage, his reserved thirty-seven-year-old wife Chrysoula had resigned herself to an unfulfilling sex life because of Dimitri's tendency to ejaculate prematurely. After thirty seconds, give or take, he'd be finished for the evening. Understandably, Chrysoula felt intensely frustrated. Then, on a shopping trip to London, Chrysoula saw a sex shop just off Bond Street and, on a whim, walked in. She was looking for a way to make sex both satisfying and fun without upsetting her husband or making him feel inadequate. When she came across a palette of edible body paints, she smiled suddenly. *"This could be fun,"* she thought to herself. *"And what do I have to lose?"*

On her flight back to Cyprus, Chrysoula thought about how she might approach this new endeavor. Dimitri may have been a cosmopolitan businessman, but his attitude in bed was all Mediterranean machismo. She knew he felt sexually unsure of himself, but also that he would be humiliated and angry if she confronted the problem directly. That night, as they got into bed, Chrysoula took the paints out of the nightstand drawer.

"Paint me," she commanded, gazing directly at her husband. "Use the apple green and start with my breasts," she went on, smearing some of the goo on her breasts to show him what she wanted. She shocked herself with her uncharacteristic behavior, yet thoroughly enjoyed the tingle of excitement that ran down her entire body.

Continuing to take the lead, Chrysoula let Dimitri know when he could get physical—he was not to touch himself or rub against her in any way until she encouraged him. She used gentle monosyllables to guide him: "the nipple, harder, circles, tongue." Dimitri was hesitant at first, but soon began to follow his wife's directions with enthusiasm. For the first time ever, they experienced simultaneous orgasms. By trying something radically different—reversing roles and becoming playful—Chrysoula and Dimitri found a new and satisfying way to connect. Dimitri, who was responsible for a staff of twenty-five at the bank and had shouldered a tremendous amount of responsibility, discovered an arena where he could relax, do as he was told, and enjoy the ride.

Esther Perel, M.A., a professor in the Department of Psychiatry at New York University, has a provocative "outsider" perspective on American sex lives. Born and raised in Belgium, she believes that some of America's most treasured values—equality, collaboration, and communication—just don't work that well in the bedroom. "Sexual desire doesn't play by the same rules of good citizenship that maintain peace and contentment between partners," Perel says. "Sexual excitement is politically incorrect."

# WHEN NAUGHTY IS NICE

MONIQUE IS A slim, attractive thirty-two-year-old French homemaker and mother of two daughters. After ten years of marriage, Monique and Eduoard's sex life had become predictable and somewhat monotonous—a twice-a-week chore, almost akin to doing the laundry. But instead of giving up, Monique started dressing up. She laughs as she remembers her first endeavor.

"I borrowed a girlfriend's nurse's outfit and I left the bathroom light on so I was illuminated upon opening the bedroom door. It was very dramatic."

"Yes," Eduoard concurred laughingly, "she looked like an angel."

Now, every Wednesday is Monique's night to dress up in a costume of her choice. "It breaks up the week," she said with a smile, "and our favorites often come back for a repeat performance."

Eduoard loves their erotic ritual. "I'm on the edge of my seat every Wednesday night through dinner. I can't wait for the kids to go to bed. . . . I never know what awaits me."

A few months into their ongoing costume drama, Eduoard

turned the tables on Monique, dressing up as a swashbuckling pirate. Now he surprises her every Saturday evening.

"I am not as elaborate as Monique," he admits. "Sometimes my outfit is very simple, like black boots and matching satin underwear. But I always make the same entrance from the bathroom. It's the anticipation for both of us that is so exciting." And recently, they shared their erotic secret. "We told my brother and his wife what we were doing—and now my brother's night for dressing up is Sunday," he laughs. "We often trade costumes."

Nearly one third of U.S. women and one sixth of men suffer from "low sexual desire," according to a recent survey in the *Journal of the American Medical Association*. U.S. sex therapists report "death of desire" as the single most frequent problem they treat.

# GETTING OLDER, GETTING BETTER

THE CITY OF Rio is simply *very* sexual. Miles of beach is built into the metropolitan area, where tanned Brazilian women, heading to the beach, parade the boardwalk in designer bikinis and stiletto heels. Men assertively stare, wink, lick their lips, and smile. The result is a sexually charged atmosphere that continues "twenty-four seven"—nonstop, all day, everyday.

Jan, an American friend, and I were sitting in a café mid-afternoon under an umbrella, taking a break from the beach and the sun. The café balcony was set up in tiers so we had a great view of the beach and the passing crowd. Directly in front of and below us were two well-groomed and elegantly clad women in their sixties, both with large brimmed hats on, sipping juice and eating salads. Two men to our left, who were in their seventies, were staring at the women, but because of their seating area, were unable to make their interests known. One of the men called over the waiter and whispered in his ear. The other man quickly pulled a comb out of his pocket and ran it through his wispy white hair. The waiter smiled and nodded.

The men gathered their belongings and moved down one level to the table next to the women. One of the men smiled and leaned toward the woman next to him, extending his hand. She took his hand and he gingerly kissed her fingertips. She giggled. He then closed his eyes and rubbed her hand on his cheek. The other man leaped out of his seat and swung his chair to the other side of the table to be near the other woman. They amiably chatted for several minutes and then the two couples left arm-in-arm for a stroll down the beach.

"Now that was amazing," Jan said.

"Absolutely," I said, "to be mature and be so smooth!"

"To the golden years," Jan pledged.

"Amen," I responded. We laughed and clinked our juice glasses.

> In a study by Sergio Luis de Freitas, a Brazilian psychologist, gerontologist, and founder of the *Journal of Sexology,* approximately seventy-four percent of retired Brazilians still had sex, with nearly half of them having sex at least twice per week.

# INTERNATIONAL UNMENTIONABLES

I WAS IN Paris on a short layover and called Pierre, a new friend I'd met at a party on a previous layover. We agreed to meet in the afternoon for a stroll around the city and catch up over dinner. Meeting at the Metro, we zipped over to the Université de Paris and walked toward the Arc de Triomphe and the Champs d'Elysée. Pierre always wants to practice his English while I, of course, prefer to practice my French, so we simply swap languages for the day.

"Perfect," Pierre said, "ze best street for shopeeng."

*"Mais oui,"* I responded, *"c'est magnifique."* We looked at each other and laughed.

"I need some seengs," he said haltingly.

*"Pookwa paaas?"* I responded, throwing my hands up as we both chuckled again.

As we passed a lingerie store, I saw Pierre's eyes light up. He motioned me to follow him as we cut through the crowded street into the packed store. Men, women, and couples were lined up in the narrow aisles around countless bins of loosely stacked underwear, holding small metal baskets stacked with designated purchases. A woman in front of me held up a pair of black lace hose, complete with a missing crotch, and smiled at her companion. *"Oui, oui,"* he said with eyes ablaze.

Feeling uncomfortable and forgetting our deal to speak each other's language, I tapped Pierre on the shoulder. "I'll wait over here," I said, and motioned toward the door. As Pierre shopped, I stood hunched by the doorway with my hands in my pockets. I thought about my basic white briefs and T-shirts and how those biannual purchases are, for me, more of a chore than an adventure.

Finally, I sheepishly walked toward one of the bins closest to me and picked up a pair of black silk men's underwear. The briefs were cut high on the side with what appeared to be a padded crotch. Dropping the underwear back into the bin, I shook my head. "I just don't see it," I mumbled to myself.

Turning back to the doorway, I saw Pierre, holding two bags of purchases, smiling. He's seen me looking at the silk bikini.

"Get it, you conservatif Americaaan," he said and we both fell over laughing. I felt my face flush and I couldn't speak. "Come on," he prodded. "Just try eet. You'll like eet!" I succumbed to peer pressure and bought the underwear. I must admit, they are very comfortable and make me feel . . . well, hot!

A 2002 study by the French Market Research Institute, in cooperation with the department store Galleries Lafayette, found that a whopping eighty-seven percent of the French population characterize lingerie as an important part of life.

# GOING SOLO BEFORE YOU FLY

GILLIAN, A VOLUPTUOUS thirty-eight-year-old British flight attendant friend with porcelain skin and wavy brown hair, has long been at war with her body. After winning a string of beauty pageants as a child and teenager, then being forced to adhere to strict weight requirements for her airline employer, she felt liberated once the weight restrictions for flight attendants were lifted in the mid-1990s. She quickly gained twenty-five pounds as a result of discovering ice cream and candy bars—two foods that had been off-limits to her for most of her life. The result: she felt sexually unattractive and began to avoid her husband's overtures.

"I knew I couldn't go on like that—I mean, how big was I going to get?" She said. "But I also knew I wasn't going to deprive myself ever again to be a size four." In addition to pledging to a healthier diet, Gillian wanted to get comfortable with her body just as it was. "So I bought a series of vibrators," she said smiling at the memory. "I knew I could get my groove back and feel sexy again—regardless of my weight."

Gillian took her toys on her international layovers and played in her hotel room. "I would bring a bottle of champagne and run a bubble bath, setting the mood for a wonderful, hours-long self-love session," she recalled dreamily. "Eventually I would fantasize that I would order room service and my husband would be the room-service delivery person, dressed up in native costume, with a bowl full of chocolate-covered strawberries that he rubbed all over me." She giggled, "That *really* worked for me." Gillian returned home from her trips like a lioness.

As Gillian and her husband lay in bed after a particularly passionate lovemaking session, she stroked her husband's chest playfully and whispered, "I've met someone else." Her husband bolted upright, aghast. Gillian giggled. "Relax, Luv," she said gently lowering him back down onto the bed. "You know I have eyes only for you—*except* when it comes to Mr. Happy." Then she reached into her nightstand and pulled out a vibrator and seductively turned it on. Ignoring her husband's stammers, Gillian ran the vibrator all over her body, from her toes, up her thigh, along her sides, and encircling her breasts. Eventually Gillian's husband started playing with Mr. Happy too. It was the beginning of a beautiful three-way relationship—one they still enjoy today.

According to a 2004 study by Dr. Laura Berman, a sex therapist and professor at Northwestern University, women who use sexual devices report higher levels of sexual desire and arousal than those who don't use sexual devices. In addition, nine out of ten study participants report being comfortable talking to their partners about their sexual-device use and most do not consider sexual devices a replacement for their partner, but rather a complement to their sex lives.

# BERLIN BODIES

BERLIN IS A picturesque city in transition. Rick, an airline friend, and I stayed in Mitte, an evolving part of East Berlin. There are hip boutiques with multicolored terra cotta, peach, and golden facades next to traditional solid apartments with rod-iron balconies and arched windows. We passed by Checkpoint Charlie and found eerie sections of the Berlin Wall still standing with barbed wire in front.

Rick and I were looking through some tourist literature when he said "Hey, let's go to the Sex Museum." I furrowed my brow, envisioning a porn show. But when Rick read the description, it sounded interesting—a museum full of sex-related artifacts from around the world, including ancient Chinese and Japanese prints in various love positions, Indian couple figurines engaged in love acts, and paintings of Persian harems. The ad for the museum was featured alongside the other city tourist attractions.

"It sounds like it's on the up and up," I conceded. "Let's go."

When we arrived at the location, we exchanged worried looks. The building looked a bit run-down and stood between two porn establishments. "Well, it's just a few bucks," Rick said, "and we took the trouble of finding it." Apprehensively, we walked in.

To my delight, the museum interior was very inviting—soothing magenta walls, cool lighting, and relaxing New Age music. Placards clearly described each piece in German, French, and English. Although the museum was crowded, it was hushed. But the most startling part of our visit was the reaction of the crowd: the men, women, couples, and children seriously surveyed the artwork, just like attendees at any museum.

A German family of five—parents, two teenage girls, and a younger brother—entered directly in front of us, and our paths repeatedly crossed as we made our way through the museum. The father pointed to a male figurine with an exceptionally large crotch and made a comment that elicited a relaxed chuckle from his children. Then the mother, stroking her cheek, took a special interest in a light floral Asian tapestry and shared a few words with her family.

Rick looked at me and whispered, "This is very different and not remotely lewd or uncomfortable."

"Yes," I said, "I find this very interesting."

According to the *Washington Post,* the Berlin Sex Museum attracts a quarter of a million visitors annually and ranks among the city's top five museums in attendance. Europe also features sex museums in Amsterdam, Barcelona, and Copenhagen.

# FRANCOPHILE FUNDAMENTALS

As I sat in a café near the Pompidou Centre in Paris with my French friends Jean-Luc and Martine, who are parents of sixteen-year-old twin girls, our conversation turned to sex. I asked them their secret to raising sexually responsible children.

"Oh, *mon dieu,*" Jean-Luc gasped, nervously running his hands through his hair. "They will always be my little girls in my mind," he admitted, "but they are young adults now, non?" Shrugging, he continued, "I don't know if we have a secret, but Martine and I, and probably most of the French, believe that one of the main responsibilities of a parent is to provide our children with information and guidance. Our children quickly become adults and we have to make that transition with them, so they can make educated decisions. We have always been open with our bodies as a family, but discussing sex with my girls, it was not easy for me at the beginning . . ."

Laughing, Martine added, "It was difficult for both of us, but more so for Jean-Luc. But I insisted we do it together and we have answered the girls' questions as they've matured."

"Many years ago, when Nadine was this high," Jean-Luc said signaling with his hands just above his knees, "she came into our bedroom while we were making love." Jean-Luc said. "Nadine looked at us and said, 'What are you doing?'" Martine and Jean-Luc burst into laughter. "So I took a deep breath and told her," he said.

"It gets easier over time" Martine explained. "The more comfortable we are, the more comfortable they are."

"Seriously," Martine said and her smile dissipating, "I want our girls to be as comfortable talking about sex with their father as they are talking with me," Martine went on. "About four years ago, one of our daughters started her period when I was out of town visiting my sister. She felt comfortable going to Jean-Luc, confiding in him and seeking his support. Of course we have twins, so I knew our other daughter would not be far behind. But I didn't feel the need to cut my trip short and run home. At that moment, I knew we had done our job well."

> The University of North Carolina at Charlotte reports that among American teenagers ages eighteen and nineteen, nearly half had two or more sexual partners in the last year. Among eighteen- to nineteen-year-olds in France, fewer than thirteen percent of French girls and twenty-nine percent of French boys had two or more sexual partners last year.

# NO-DRAMA DUTCH

AFTER SPENDING ALL day in Amsterdam's fascinating Reichs Museum, I sat sipping a Heineken at an outdoor café as the crowd sauntered by. A group of kids across the street were lining up for a movie. "That's Matt!" I thought to myself, leaning forward in my chair. The teenager turned and after catching another view of his profile, I realized it wasn't him after all. I started to think about Matt and realized he would now be much older than the young man across the street.

Years ago, when I was a grad student in Chicago, I volunteered one night a week at a local community center as a mentor for teenagers, ages thirteen to seventeen, who wanted to "drop in" and chat with an adult for support and guidance. Sixteen-year-old Matt, one of the kids who came every week, was one of my favorites. Clean-cut and smiling, he lived in Evanston, an upscale suburb just north of Chicago. Matt was a big Northwestern football fan and since I was a Purdue grad and booster, we often talked about the games and "high-fived" each other after one of our teams won. Then one week Matt showed up dazed and grim, his eyes brimming with tears. "My penis is burning and it has a cut," he told me miserably. "One of my friends said I probably have herpes."

When I urged Matt to consult with his parents, he reluctantly agreed but only if I went with him. And off to Evanston we went—for one of the longest one-hour visits in my life. After brief introductions, Matt's parents, Matt, and I sat stiffly around the kitchen table. Matt's chin was on his chest as the tears ran off his cheeks. "I think I have herpes," he mumbled.

"What?" his father shouted.

Matt's mother stood trembling with rage. "How could you let this happen?" she shrieked. "No, don't tell me, I don't want to know," she said bitterly as she stormed out of the room. From the other side of the house, we heard her spit out: "You're grounded . . . forever!" Matt fled to his room.

After a moment of excruciating silence, I said, "I think I should be going." As Matt's father raised his hand in a half-hearted attempt to wave, he started to cry. I never saw Matt or his family again.

I wondered if circumstances would have been different for Matt if he had been raised in Holland. According to nonprofit organization Advocates For Youth, adults in the Netherlands, France, and Germany view young people as assets, not as problems. In Europe, sex education is not only discussed at home, but is an integral part of the school curriculum. In fact, a 2004 study by the Joint United Nations Program on HIV/AIDS found that sex education did not increase sexual activity among teens, and in some cases, actually delayed it, reducing the number of sexual partners.

A study by the University of North Carolina at Charlotte reports the U.S. teenage gonorrhea rate alone is seventy-four times higher than the rates in Holland and France. In addition, the HIV prevalence rate in young men ages fifteen to twenty-four is over five times higher than the rate in Germany.

# 7

# Good GRIEF

# RELEASE AND RELIEF

I FELT LIKE taking a trip on my own and after reading a fascinating article in *Travel and Leisure*, I opted for Syria. I decided to bypass the busy capital of Damascus and take a step back in time by going directly to Aleppo, the oldest continuously inhabited city in the world. The ancient city boasts the Citadel, a huge, coliseum-like fortress, as well as hundreds of other historic buildings. Throughout the city are noisy, tarp-covered souks (open-air markets) with terrific bargains on a huge array of goods, from copper and leather to mother-of-pearl inlaid wood and naturally moisturizing, homemade olive oil soap.

In the Christian section of Jdeide, Orthodox churches are prevalent. As I traipsed through the ancient city, I meandered into a beautiful ornate Syrian Orthodox church with a large white cross on top. Upon entering, I was awed by the amber-stained glass and the intricately painted ceilings that portrayed Jesus and an array of saints. In the front of the church was a priest draped in black vestments. Discreetly, I slid into the last pew.

As the bearded priest at the altar conducted mass, the smell of incense permeated the small church. Then, I noticed a cake at the front of the altar with some writing and dates. Although I couldn't make out the writing, I realized it must be a name because below it were the dates, March 1945–September 1995, which I assumed to be birth and death years. In the first pew sat a mourning family—a middle-aged woman in black and three men in their early twenties—all sobbing loudly.

Sitting next to me was a man consoling his wife, who cried and dabbed at her eyes with a white handkerchief. I nodded sympathetically at them.

"It's her cousin," the man whispered to me.

"I'm sorry," I responded.

"Today is the forty-day ceremony. She is better now," he added giving his companion a squeeze, "but the funeral . . ." His voice trailed off as he pursed his lips and shook his head. "The funeral was very difficult."

I knew that in addition to the funeral, the Syrian, Russian, and Greek Orthodox communities have memorial services at both forty days and one year after the death, which allows mourners to revisit their loss and thus continue the healing process.

I was baptized Greek Orthodox and although I am not aligned with any one particular religion, I remember that my father's forty-day service was very helpful to me. My father's death traumatized me. I had the deepest respect for his integrity, honesty, intelligence, compassion, sense of humor, and, in particular, his zest for life. We had a great rapport, and I loved him deeply. When I lost him, I lost one of my best friends.

Initially, I had an emotionless reaction to my father's death. Some of this was probably denial, but I also remember feeling that I had to keep a stiff upper lip and not let anybody see me falter. Those around me kept saying "you have to be strong" whenever my eyes started to tear or my lips started to quiver. But by keeping grief inside, I made myself ill. I couldn't eat or sleep and my body ached all over. Finally, five weeks after the funeral, on the night of the forty-day memorial service, while relaxing at home, I succumbed. Sounds erupted from the depths of my soul; I screamed and thrashed, pounding my fist on the walls. Then, exhausted, I fell asleep. When I awoke, I felt strangely lighter and more peaceful. I knew that my healing had begun.

According to Elizabeth Kubler Ross, the celebrated author of *On Death and Dying,* most people have to go through several stages of mourning including denial, anger, bartering, and depression in order to heal and move on from any significant loss. Many studies indicate that fully experiencing and expressing one's grief aids in the healing process.

# VIETNAMESE FAREWELL

MY FRIENDS REGINE and Thomas were having a wonderful time on the outskirts of Saigon. "It seemed like everyday we learned something fascinating about the culture, from weddings to funerals," Regine told me.

On the third day of their vacation, they came across a huge sobbing group on one of the main suburban streets.

"Somebody important must have died," Regine whispered to her husband. Curious, they joined the procession. Within seconds, they were enveloped by the moving stream and were surrounded by sporadic screams and wails.

"I am feeling claustrophobic," Regine said to Thomas as she held on to his sleeve. He steered her out of the crowd, and they made their way to the side of the street with other onlookers.

"What is happening?" Thomas asked one of the spectators, a young woman in her twenties. She shrugged and Thomas wasn't sure if she didn't know or couldn't speak English. The burgeoning procession now numbered in the hundreds, which piqued Thomas's curiosity even more.

"Do you speak English?" Thomas asked the man next to him.

"Yes," he responded smiling.

"Somebody famous must have died," Thomas said motioning at the weeping crowd.

The man nodded, adding that the deceased owned one of the stores on the main street.

"He knew so many people," Regine observed. "He must have been very well liked."

The man smiled. "All of these people," he said motioning to the mob in front of them, "have been paid by the family." he said.

"Well," Regine said, slipping her hand around her husband's waist, "I certainly hope he's looking down and appreciating their efforts!" she said.

After Regine relayed her experience to me, we agreed to cherish important people in our lives while they are here. We decided to either call or write the ten closest people in our lives and tell them how much we love them. It was a wonderful experience.

---

According to Ann Cadell Crawford, a cultural consultant to the U.S. government, it is vital in Vietnam to appropriately and respectfully mourn family members at death. Family members often hire professional mourners to attend their relative's funeral because a proper and well-attended funeral honors the family name.

# TANZANIAN GOOD-BYES

My friend Phil is the son of Mennonite missionaries. He was raised in Tanzania, and loves to reminisce about his childhood. His eyes soften whenever he discusses the beauty of Africa's highest mountain, Mount Kilimanjaro, and the wildebeests, zebras, and gazelles that inhabit the plains of the Serengeti. He told me about the Eden-like island of Zanzibar, with its pristine beaches, lush forest reserves, and abundant plantations that grew vegetables, fruit, and spices. "There's a reason that Dr. Livingston called Zanzibar 'the finest place I have ever known in all of Africa,'" he said.

Phil also told me about the strong spiritual conviction of the Tanzanian people and how that belief system helped people cope with the day-to-day struggles of life. "Africa seems to deal with one relentless crisis after another, from starvation to disease to AIDS," he said shaking his head.

"How do they deal with it all," I wondered aloud.

"Faith," Phil said. "Faith that what happens in life is God's will and the life path for each individual is simply what is meant to be." Phil then told me about a story an American teacher friend relayed to him. When the teacher met her student in the hallway, she offered her condolences to him. The student's child had recently passed away from a bout of pneumonia. The student shrugged and replied *"Mungu Yuko Tu"*—"God is." Remembering local protocol, the American teacher responded *"Eeh, ni kweli"*—"It's true." The student then broke into a broad smile upon receiving the reassurance he needed.

> "It is by God's action that he or she died."—Swahili proverb

# KOREAN GOOD-BYES

CHRIS, A LONG-TIME friend and former roommate, was a station manager for a large American airline on Guam. In addition to being responsible for his own airline operations, he and his staff represented the ground operations of other carriers, who had a smaller presence on Guam. One of those carriers was a Korean airline.

The Korean jumbo jet, full of tourists on holiday, was on final approach to land on Guam on a particularly foggy day when the aircraft slammed into a mountain a mile short of the runway. Chris and his team kicked into emergency response mode and were devastated to discover that hundreds of people had been killed in the crash.

The Korean airline representatives from Seoul told Chris that they were sending an additional aircraft with families of the victims to Guam. An hour before the scheduled aircraft was to land, Chris felt his stomach churn. What would he face in the next couple of hours?

As they assembled in the Customs Hall, the families were tearful but eerily quiet. The translators kept repeating the same message to Chris: The crowd wanted to know how quickly they could go to the crash site. Chris looked out the window at a relentless storm. It was the middle of monsoon season and heavy rains were expected to continue for days. Chris explained to the interpreter that they would have to wait until the weather improved, but that the group would be kept comfortable in a hotel until that time. When the Korean translator's lips tightened, Chris was gripped with dread.

When the translator explained the delay to the waiting group, the quiet, polite Koreans lost control. Women bellowed while men fell to their knees, slamming the ground with their hands. A teenager started to scream and slam his head against the wall. Directly in front of Chris, a group screamed at him with outstretched arms.

"What are they saying?" Chris shouted to the translator, backing away from the crowd.

"They say you have abandoned them and that their families are all alone in the rain."

Chris sprang into action. He and his team worked for the next several hours to devise a different routing to get the family members to the crash site.

"Once they were there, they were fine," Chris recalled. "They just had to be together at the spot where their loved ones took their last breath, and know they could bring them home."

As Chris described his experience to me, I shivered. In 1994, I was scheduled to be on a plane that crashed. At the last minute, my plans changed and I took an earlier flight that day from Chicago to Pittsburgh. My family, however, didn't know my plans had changed and assumed I was on the ill-fated airliner. When I heard about the crash, I called my parents, who had already seen the news on television. I'll never forget my dad's reaction when he picked up the phone and heard my voice. My typically very calm father screamed "It's Bill, it's Bill!" I heard my mother shriek and then, although not a word was said, we silently remained on the line together, crying and connected.

Koreans believe nobody should die alone.

# ISRAELI SHALOM

DAVID, AN ISRAELI classmate from graduate school, talked about his brother's unexpected passing in one of my cultural diversity classes.

"It was devastating. My brother wasn't even forty and left his two teenage boys behind." His voice broke and he took a deep breath. "Cancer," he whispered. "Three weeks after his diagnosis, he was gone."

David explained that from the moment his brother died in Tel Aviv, his family was beside him. The family buried him the day after he died and then "sat *shiva*," or mourned, for a week as friends and relatives visited the family home to pay their respects. Following tradition, David planted a simple elm tree in his yard to honor his brother. David tearfully explained that he has been able to say all the things to the tree that he never had the chance to tell his brother to his face.

"It's really a beautiful tree and it has grown so quickly and strongly," he told me. "I have leaned against the trunk many a day and just talked about life with him. I can always feel him near me."

Remembering David's story, I felt a strong urge to plant a

tree for my dad. Unfortunately, as a city dweller, I didn't and still don't have a yard. So I identified a tree in a nearby park as Dad's tree and I often find myself leaning against that tree, finding comfort and remembering him.

Three months before my father died, I coordinated a seventy-fifth birthday party for him. My intuition told me it would be Dad's last birthday. He had congestive heart failure and his once strapping 185-pound frame had been whittled down to 130 pounds. However, his smile and zest for life still shone through. After the guests had departed the party and we started to clean up, my dad put his arm around my shoulder.

"Thank you for my party," he said.

"Sure Dad," I responded. Then I turned and looked into his eyes. They were misty and I sensed he wanted to say more. I put down the dishes I was holding.

"You know I love you," he stated. "And you know I respect you," he continued.

"I . . . I know that Dad," I stammered, feeling my throat tighten.

"I just want you to know how much I have enjoyed having you as my son," he said. He gave my shoulder a squeeze. "Always know that I will be here for you," he said taking my hand. "Just look over your shoulder and I will be there."

As we hugged each other, the tears ran down my face. He gave me a big smile and my instincts told me he had carefully planned this moment. And now, when I am not sure what to do about a life decision, I go to my tree. I lean against it, talk it out, and look over my shoulder. Somehow, the decisions always come easier after that.

> During the seven days of *shiva,* the mourning period directly following the funeral, well wishers bring simple foods to the family home. This allows Jewish mourners to not concern themselves with mundane tasks like cooking, but instead to sit on boxes or low benches and focus on their grief. (Thus, the term, sitting *shiva.*)

# DAY OF THE DEAD

MY FRIEND CINDY was on the phone. "Want to go to Wahaka?"

"Do I want to what?" I responded.

"Wahaka," she explained, "is the charming artist colony in Mexico with lots of indoor and outdoor markets, filled with great shopping!" Although it was the tail end of October, not yet time for a warm weather vacation, I had some time off and it sounded like an interesting opportunity. Besides, just spending time with Cindy was always a pleasure.

"Sure, a getaway sounds great."

Oaxaca (pronounced Wahaka) is a quaint, low-key city with small roadside stands loaded with local pottery, jewelry, and rugs as well as a smattering of galleries featuring local artists. However, at this particular time of year, sleepy Oaxaca took on a whole new feel. There were skeletons hanging in doorways of homes, edible cakes in the shapes of skulls in stores, paper bones hanging from balconies, and toy coffins on porches.

I looked at Cindy and said, "Wow, I didn't know they celebrated Halloween in Mexico."

But we learned that this was no trick-or-treat holiday. Instead, November second is All Souls Day, when Mexicans honor and pay their respects to their ancestors. But the day is not mournful—it is joyful and festive. Cindy, who is fluent in Spanish, asked the taxi driver about the significance of the day as we drove back to the hotel after dinner.

"The day celebrates the continuance of life and family relationships," he said. After Cindy translated his message, the driver looked at me, bobbing his head up and down, as he smiled. *"Familia, muy important,"* he said. *"Si,"* I nodded. "Family is very important."

The next morning, Cindy, who is quite outgoing and a bit of a flirt, met a local shop owner named Ramon. He invited her to dinner that night at his family home to celebrate Day of the Dead.

"Go," I encouraged her. "It will be fascinating. Just remember everything so you can tell me!"

Cindy returned to the hotel at one AM and for several hours, we sat up and talked about her amazing evening. She described the elaborate altar set up in the home, decorated with pictures of deceased ancestors. The family enjoyed a feast: chicken in molé sauce, platters of rice and beans, candied pumpkin, and several cakes. Meals had also been prepared for each deceased ancestor, with special toys and candy set in front of the sole child's picture, who had died three years earlier of pneumonia at the age of two.

Sitting around the candlelit dining area, each family member spoke. Aunts, uncles, parents, brothers, and grandmothers talked about the relatives that had passed, bringing their special personalities to life. The great-grandmother and matriarch of the clan talked endearingly of her daughter, who had died of cancer at sixty-two.

"Maria was very funny," she said. "Full of life and always playing practical jokes." Cindy recalled how the young girl seated next to her looked up at Cindy and giggled, "That's my mom's mom she is talking about." The four-year-old leaped up from the table, ran to the altar and pointed at her grandmother's picture. Then she held onto her dress and entertainingly pulled it from side-to-side in an impromptu dance.

"My mom says I'm like her!" she blurted out and ran toward her mother, burying her head in her mother's lap. They all laughed at the child's antics as her mother picked her up, hugged her close and looked into her eyes.

"Yes," she said with a broad smile as she rocked her daughter. "You are just like her!"

Tears came to Cindy's eyes. Although she knew her own grandparents' names, she never learned what they were like as people. When people die, why do we bury our memories with them, she wondered. She pledged that when she had children, she would prepare diaries to pass on to them or find some other way to preserve memories of loved ones.

Writer Octavio Paz observed that the Mexican has no qualms about getting up close and personal with death. He "chases after it, mocks it, courts it, hugs it, sleeps with it; it is his favorite plaything and his most lasting love."

# THAI GOOD-BYE

LAURA, AN AMERICAN friend, was living and working in Bangkok and dating a young man named Tam. When Tam's mother unexpectedly passed away, he asked Laura to come home with him to his village for the ceremony.

"Can you come for the week?" Tam asked her.

"The *week*?" she repeated, flabbergasted. But looking into Tam's eyes and seeing his pain, she called her boss and made the arrangements. "What are we going to do for an entire week?" she wondered.

Upon arriving at Tam's childhood village home, a two-hour drive from Bangkok, Laura and Tam walked into a house full of family and neighbors. A sideboard was piled high with foods. Two men were playing dominoes, while a group of four others were playing cards. But Laura noticed it wasn't a party atmosphere. People spoke to each other but the mood was quiet and respectful.

Tam leaned toward Laura and whispered, "It will be like this every night for a while. They are sharing my mother's space and her company."

And it was. For four nights, the neighbors came to the house, brought food, feasted, and played games.

"The fifth night was magical," Laura recalled. All of Tam's family and friends stood together in the main room of the house holding hands. Laura stood between Tam and his aunt. When the group began to sing songs, Laura, not knowing the words or how to react, started to fidget. Tam's aunt gave Laura's hand a reassuring squeeze and they exchanged smiles.

As the others continued to sing, Tam and several of the other men went into the bedroom and took Tam's mother, in her coffin, out of the house on a splendid path of banana leaves that wound down the front stairs and through the front yard. Laura, with tears in her eyes, put her arms around Tam's tiny aunt.

"Where is she going now?" Laura asked in her limited Thai.

"Home," Tam's aunt answered.

Laura accompanied the group on foot to the local Buddhist temple where Tam's mother, surrounded by family, friends, and neighbors, was cremated.

> In Thailand, traditionally there are memorial services the seventh, fiftieth, and hundredth days after death.

# ARRIVEDERCI NONI

MY PHONE RANG in the middle of the night.

"It's Marilena," the voice whispered on the other end of the line. Marilena and I met in college and had remained very close even after she moved back to her native Italy.

"Are you okay?" I asked.

"Noni died," she said, her voice cracking. Noni was Marilena's outspoken and entertaining grandmother, to whom she had been extremely close. Marilena used to tell me hysterically funny "Noni stories" that would leave us howling with laughter. When I offered to visit, Marilena gratefully accepted. I left for Genoa that evening.

When I saw Marilena at the airport, she buried her head in my shoulder and sobbed. After a couple of minutes, she looked at me through reddened eyes and thanked me for coming. As we silently walked to her car, holding hands, she turned to me and said, "I should cry more often. I feel better."

On the way to Marilena's family home, we passed charming terra cotta and gold-hued buildings built along the sea. Small blue and white fishing boats lined tiny piers, while random rock formations jutted out of the shallow seas.

"Genoa is gorgeous," I said as we wove through the maze of narrow streets, passing palacelike homes with marble facades.

The next day, after a heavy sleep, Marilena and I took a ride on the *Bigo,* a rotating panoramic lift that offered a birds-eye view of the entire city. As we soared through the sky, Marilena started to open up. She told me about her grandmother's final two nights. She gave Noni a last kiss, held her hand, and told her how much she would miss her.

That night I joined Marilena and her somber family for "*novenas,*" a series of prayers dedicated to the memory of Noni. The next night we repeated the novena ritual and although I left the following day, Marilena explained that they would hold *novenas* for a total of nine nights following the funeral.

"On the ninth night, we hold a feast," Marilena said with a hint of a smile. "Noni will like that. She loves a party." I smiled back at Marilena.

"It's great," I retorted gripping Marilena's hand, "that you can end on a festive note. Knowing Noni, that's the way she would want it!"

Roman Catholics almost always bury the deceased. Although cremation is no longer expressly forbidden, ashes cannot typically be brought into a church for a funeral mass without special dispensation.

# GLOBAL GOOD-BYES

MY FATHER DIED in late July of 2001. Six weeks later, the tragedies of September eleventh struck and I became very depressed. Not long after that, I received a call from a Samoan friend, Lon. He told me that he, along with two other mutual friends, Amir, an Egyptian, and Toshi from Japan, would like to take me out to dinner. I hesitated.

"I'm not feeling very social these days," I told him.

"You might need to get out," Lon urged. Somewhat reluctantly, I agreed to meet my friends for dinner.

The four of us met at a local diner. Although we had never hugged before, we all embraced. It just seemed right.

"How are you doing?" Amir asked me.

"I've been better," I responded with a weak smile. Amir nodded, and we began to eat in silence. Suddenly and inexplicably, I felt like talking. I started telling my friends about Dad's funeral and how much better I felt after the forty-day memorial service.

Then Lon shared his own experience with loss. When he lost his father, following American-Samoan tradition, his family conducted the funeral service in his parent's home so that his dad could have a final visit at home with his family and friends.

"I found that really comforting," Lon told us. "It gave me a chance to say good-bye to him on his own turf."

Then Amir told us about when his grandmother died in Cairo. "I was just a kid," Amir said. "But I remember my mom giving me some of Grandma's favorite sweets to put in her coffin." His mother had explained to him that the treats would allow Grandma to enjoy her trip to heaven. "I always thought that was kind of nice," Amir recalled, smiling wistfully.

Toshi, who had lost his mother the year before but had never talked about his feelings, suddenly began to speak of her.

"My mother was cremated," he told us, "her ashes sat on an altar in our family home outside Tokyo for thirty-five days." Before anybody could respond, Toshi added, "It's tradition. We burned incense all day and night for over a month and people came to pay their respects." We were silent for a moment taking this in.

"Do people drop in and leave right away?" Amir finally asked.

"No," Toshi responded. "They burn an incense stick and spend time with us." At the end of the mourning period, Toshi told us that his family said their final good-byes and they buried the urn. "I visit her when I go home every year, and I know my dad and sister visit her often," he said. "I miss her," he added, wiping away a tear.

Silently, I patted him on the shoulder and we quietly finished our dinners. Then Amir told us about the experience of his Irish girlfriend, Meg, at her grandfather's funeral. "It was a party," he said. "Everybody went to a local bar and took turns reminiscing about her grandfather. It was almost like a celebration."

As we parted ways with another round of hugs, I looked at each of my friends in turn.

"Thanks for getting me back out into the world," I said. On the way home, I thought about all of the different ways we mourn loved ones who have passed.

There are many **paths** that take us to the same **loving** place.

# 8
# Expanding Your Comfort ZONE

# INFILTRATING IRAN?

WHEN I WAS fourteen and living in Greece, I was walking to football practice one afternoon with one of my friends, Jim, when he turned to me and said, "My dad says your dad is with the CIA." I had never thought about this before. *Could it be true?* My dad was on a business trip at the time, but I resolved to ask him about it as soon as he got home.

The following week, as our family was finishing dinner, I casually said, "Dad, Jim's dad thinks you're a spy." I looked at Mom for a reaction, but there wasn't one.

"Does he really?" my dad responded with a smile. "Have you got a roof over your head and food in your tummy?" he asked jovially. He got up from the table and tousled my hair. "Then you have nothing to worry about."

"Okay," I said, relieved that there appeared to be nothing to the rumor.

Twenty years later, in my midthirties, I read an article on the CIA that claimed one out of three Americans living overseas had links to the intelligence community. Dad spoke four languages fluently and had a working knowledge of several others. Every time our family moved to a different country, my dad worked for a different U.S. company—from RCA to Singer to STP. Were these merely covers? Moreover, he was very intuitive, possessing an uncanny ability to pick up what was going on around him at all times. I remember tending bar at one of the cocktail parties my parents hosted. After the party, as my parents and I conversed about the guests, I wondered how my dad knew so many details of the conversations going on around him while remaining so immersed in the conversation he was having with his own group.

*No, it couldn't be,* I said to myself. My dad was such a kind, gentle soul. The thought of him in clandestine operations seemed almost laughable. Once again, I dismissed the thought.

Four years ago, a year before Dad passed away, he had an operation to install a pacemaker. After the operation, I sat with him in his hospital room. Dad wanted to talk. For almost seven hours, he recounted many of his life and travel experiences, some of which I'd heard before, but most of which I had not. He told me about some amazing experiences, like the time he was in the Shah of Iran's royal palace in Tehran with an RCA coworker, installing the Shah's new television service. He described the beautiful, opulent rooms and remembered how rough and "peasantlike" the Shah's mother was, constantly screaming at the servants.

"Dad, *you* wired a television?" I asked incredulously. My dad was never a handyman, and it seemed so out of character.

"There's a lot you don't know about your old man," he said with a smile. Then I sat transfixed as he told me about a trip flying into Doha, Qatar, part of the United Arab Emirates, in a four-seater single propeller plane during a sandstorm, with just him and one pilot onboard. He sat beside the pilot as they lost sight of the runway every few seconds on final approach. After a harrowing landing, he met up with a British group who took him to a small hotel where he gratefully enjoyed a couple of beers.

"Who were you working for then?" I asked him.

"Singer," he said. I laughed. "How many sewing machines were you planning to sell there?" I asked. Dad just smiled and moved on to the next memory.

On the way home that evening, I wondered if I really knew my dad at all. Then I came to the realization that I knew the parts of my dad that I needed to know. He was supportive, loving, and made my brothers and I priorities. We all have parts of our lives that are private. Suddenly, it didn't really matter if he was involved in intelligence or not. He was my dad.

| |
|---|
| The best part of getting older is that you have more memories. |

# CLEANSING CHANTS

MARK AND I were seated next to each other on a flight to Buenos Aires. A dark-haired man in his midforties, he emanated a glowing, calming presence. When I commented on his level of serenity, he chuckled. "I certainly wasn't always this way," he smiled. "Nepal changed me."

As we flew south, Mark told me that he had always felt spiritually unconnected from the religion into which he was born. "It was guilt-ridden and negative," he said, adding that he knew, instinctively, that he needed to find a spiritual philosophy that was more positive and loving. He had read about Buddhism and planned a trek to Nepal to explore the religion. Landing in Katmandu, the capital city of Nepal, he was instantly mesmerized by the simplicity of the people, who, following Buddhist ways, lived lives of love, compassion, and joy. On Mark's first day there, a Nepalese couple gingerly approached Mark and silently handed him a flower. The couple nodded and walked away. "It was like coming home for me," he recalled with a smile.

Mark found the ornate Asian temples captivating, each with a series of smaller roofs leading upward to a delicately pointed top. During a walk, Mark heard a series of "ohms" emanating from inside a nearby temple. "I was curious about what was going on," he said. "Plus I knew I wanted to chant too."

The next morning Mark entered the temple wearing a long robe he had purchased the day before. Alongside other attendees, he sat cross-legged on the floor of the temple. When the group started to chant and Mark simply watched and listened for the first few minutes. Then, imitating the other worshippers, he closed his eyes and rested his hands on his thighs, palms up, with his thumb and index finger connected. "Chanting requires a lot of energy and breath from deep within," Mark told me. "I felt the negative energy and stress trapped in my body leave me, which created space to let positive, loving energy in." Mark explained the Buddhist principle that all people are connected and that all of our actions in life have consequences.

"So, in essence, we reap what we sow," I recapped.

"That's karma," he smiled and nodded.

In addition to "ohm," the mantra of joy, Mark learned other chants that promoted longevity and health. Deeply moved by his experiences, Mark decided to extend his stay. He joined a group of foreign travelers through the Himalayas, traveling with his own yak loaded up with hiking gear. Every morning Mark chanted and filled his body with crisp, clean mountain air and positive thoughts about humanity. "Since returning to the States, I have embraced a simple, somewhat spartan life," he told me. "My happiness comes from treating all people I encounter—from service people in stores to neighbors on the street—with compassion and honesty from my heart."

I liked what Mark had to say. I, too, believe that my satisfaction in life is dictated by how I treat others. Many facets of other religions, including the gentle and peaceful ways of Buddhism, appeal to me. I consider myself a "cafeteria–style" spiritualist, picking and choosing aspects of various spiritual approaches that resonate and fulfill me. But what they share in common is a focus away from materialism and on the deeper rewards of loving and sharing with others.

> *Need little, want less.*
> —Tao philosophy

# CHINESE HEALTH

MY FRIENDS TONY and Maggie, who have been dating for several months, recently visited China. In Beijing, they solemnly traced the protester's steps in Tiananmen Square and later in the day, drove north along a part of the massive expanse of the Great Wall. Dodging the zipping motorcycles, they explored the endless array of small kiosks and stalls that blanket Beijing, selling everything from fruits and vegetables to batteries and festive streamers. At sunset, as the couple meandered back to their hotel, they suddenly heard the sound of pounding drums. Around the corner appeared a long-curving snake line of women, all in synchronized steps and arm movements, holding multicolored streamers. Alongside them, a group of men drummed to an upbeat tempo and the parade became louder.

But Maggie couldn't enjoy the festivities. After a long day of sightseeing, she felt exhausted. She had long suffered from sinus infections, and after years of taking increasingly ineffective antibiotics, she had reluctantly resigned herself to a lifetime of headaches and lackluster energy. On her miserable fifth day in Beijing and preparing to head for Shanghai, she finally sought the assistance of the hotel check-in clerk. "Is there anybody that can help me for this?" she pleaded running her hands across her forehead and rocking her hands back and forth on her scalp.

The clerk referred Maggie to a nearby acupuncturist. "I wasn't keen on the needle approach," she told me later, "but I was willing to try anything." Carefully, the acupuncturist placed a needle in the center of Maggie's forehead and one at the top of each of her cheeks. "It was almost instantaneous," she recalled. "I had fluid pouring out of my nose as the acupuncturist applied light pressure at different locations on my face." Tracy was headache-free and full of energy for the rest of the trip. Better yet, she didn't have another bout with sinusitis for over six months.

Many years ago, when I was living in Chicago, attending graduate school, I had a similarly positive experience with Eastern medicine. As I was limping into class one day, my classmates rushed over asking if I needed help. I told them about the relentless pain in the top of my right foot, just below my second toe, making walking nearly unbearable. My doctor had told me that I had a foot ailment that would require surgery. "But," I told my classmates, "I just have a gut feeling that surgery is not the answer."

Ning, one of my classmates, a slim, soft-spoken Chinese man with an infectious smile, nodded thoughtfully as I spoke. He asked me if I had ever tried alternative medicine and my initial thought was "No way." But then, realizing that Western medicine had given me no relief and could only offer me risky surgery, I took Ning up on his offer to set up a visit for me. That afternoon, I hopped into a cab with his referral in hand.

As I opened the door to the small holistic center, stringed bells of old-world brass quietly chimed. I found myself in a small shop lined with shelves holding teas, oils, and bottles of lotions on the wall. From the back of the room, a small, smiling Asian man strode toward me nodding and speaking Chinese. I gave him the list of symptoms Ning had written in Chinese and he motioned me toward a back room where I sat on the edge of a bed and took off my shoes and socks. After examining my foot, he applied intense pressure to different spots around the injured spot and massaged the area—for two full hours! The excruciating pain turned into a "good hurt" and I noticed that my foot felt hot. The healer made a phone call and then, after speaking for a few moments, handed the phone to me. Ning relayed to me the healer's findings: I had calcium building up around the joints, restricting blood flow and energy. He explained how regular acupressure would bring healing energy to the spot.

But nine visits later, I started to become disillusioned. Was this *really* going to work? Although my foot always felt better after a session with "Dr. Wong," the pain would invariably return the next day. But at the end of the tenth visit, I felt the hard nodule in my foot start to give way. I could actually feel something crumbling at the base of my toes. The doctor, nodding excitedly, smiling and speaking in a fast tempo, manually dissolved the small mass. I walked out of the office a little sore from the furious rub, but no longer in pain. When I arrived home, there was a message from Ning on my machine advising me to drink as much water as I could handle that evening to flush out my system. To this day, ten years later, I haven't had a problem with my foot. And I avoided surgery!

I am now a convert. I go for a regular, preventative, deep-tissue pressure-point massage at a Chinese health center near my home, a process that releases healing energy throughout my body. After every session, I feel terrific! My stress and tension melt away, leaving me feeling physically aligned and mentally centered. No pills, no side effects, no physical invasion, nothing artificial. Only a totally natural and highly effective regimen that keeps me relaxed, energetic, and pain-free.

In 1998, the U.S. government acknowledged the credibility of alternative medicinal approaches and established the National Center for Complementary and Alternative Medicine (NCCAM), a part of the National Institute for Health (NIH).

# *BULA, BULA*

VERNON IS A cocoa-skinned African American friend who went to Fiji on vacation. As the small plane banked to land at Yasawa Island, Vernon gasped. It was a bona fide tropical paradise, with aqua water and small, thatched-roof bungalows surrounded by billowing palm trees. "Oh my God, it's Fantasy Island!" Vernon exclaimed.

Stepping off the turboprop, he was engulfed by the wet heat. Located on the equator in the middle of the Pacific, Fiji is typically in the nineties. But relief was on the way: native Fijians with sarongs approached the arriving passengers with bottled water. Vernon noticed two locals doting on an elderly couple and helping them out of the heat. *"That's nice,"* Vernon thought to himself. After receiving his bottle, Vernon smiled and thanked the young islander.

*"Bula, bula,"* the man responded, smiling, bowing as he backing away. The airline employee on the tarmac noticed Vernon's perplexed look. Putting his arm around Vernon's shoulders, he said, "'*Bula, bula*' means 'welcome, welcome!'"

The next morning Vernon explored the island, wandering through small paths and past tropical gardens. He looked ahead at grass-covered mountains and some of the most breathtaking sunrises he had ever seen. But Vernon wanted to get into the main town and meet the locals. Smiles were evident as people said "*bula*" to him as he passed.

As he walked through the town, Vernon noticed a great amount of attention being shown to elder members. People assisted elders down the street, opened doors for them, and carried their packages. Every time he initiated a conversation with a group in English or through the courtesy of a translator, Vernon noticed that the group deferred the question to the oldest group member. When he asked the tour guide about this trend, the tour guide responded, "Of course, the oldest are the most experienced and the wisest. We honor them."

Vernon was touched. "I thought about how nice that would be and something to look forward to as we age," he told me. Vernon's thoughts resonated with me. I thought about how youth-oriented our culture is and how we often cast the elderly to the side. I decided to make a more concerted effort to tap into the wisdom of previous generations by spending more time with my older relatives. By setting that precedent, I hope that the same courtesy will be extended to me in the upcoming years.

| Like a fine bottle of wine, we get better with age. |
|---|

# STANDARDS OR BIAS?

MELITA, A FEISTY, energetic Venezuelan friend, has been living in New York City for four years after graduating from college in Caracas. She is intelligent, verging on brilliant, with a passionate soul and the ability to transform convoluted ideas into clear-cut logical ones. Currently, she works in a prestigious museum in the city, but she dreams of going to law school. Although she graduated at the top of her class in Caracas, she has repeatedly done poorly on the LSAT exam in the United States. After two years of applying, she could not get accepted into any of the three law schools of her choice.

"I am so frustrated," she told me glumly. "Maybe I just don't measure up."

Feeling my lips tighten in protest, I reached out and put my hand on her arm. "Melita, you are one of the most intelligent people I know," I said. I told her about my experience as a child returning to the United States from Pakistan, when my teachers wanted to keep me back a grade because I was unfamiliar with American culture and knowledge. "My guess is that you are being tested on material you may not have been exposed to," I said.

Nodding, she said, "I did not learn much of the English grammar and sentence structure that is tested on the exam." She looked at me pleadingly. "But what can I do?"

I suggested that Melita write her essay for admission based on the whole truth about her situation, not simply on her resume. "It's not an excuse," I said. "It is simply the reality."

Melita wrote a brilliant essay, acknowledging her lack of exposure to the concepts underlying the LSAT exam, but at the same time, highlighting the unique contributions she would bring to the school based on her international upbringing and experiences. Six weeks later, I received a call from Melita. "Oh Bill, Bill, I got in, I got in!" she screamed.

The tears ran down my cheeks as I shared her excitement. "Melita, I knew you could do it!" The next evening we celebrated over dinner, toasting Melita's dream to become a defense attorney who would represent members of the Latin community.

Afterward, I thought about Melita's dilemma. *How fair are standardized tests and standardized for whom?*

According to the Law School Admission Council, only seven percent of U.S. lawyers are African American, Asian American, Latino, or Native American.

# GREEK DRINK

WHEN I WAS thirteen, my family took a summer vacation to the green, lush Greek island of Thassos, located between Greece and Turkey. After a lengthy drive from Athens, we took a small ferryboat from the mainland and arrived at a quaint family seashore resort. We were lucky: the family in the bungalow next door to us had kids the same ages as us. The days were filled with fun, snorkeling and playing in warm waters. By the end of the week, our families had bonded and on our last evening, we all went to a small Greek *taverna* for a celebratory meal.

After being seated, we walked into the kitchen to peruse that day's delicacies and I ordered *pastitsio,* a type of Greek lasagna with a delicious béchamel sauce. Once seated again, the father of my friends asked his kids if they wanted wine. They casually responded that they did. "I want wine too," I said with a smirk, not really expecting my parents to allow it.

They exchanged glances and then, my dad hesitantly agreed. "Wine is to be sipped and enjoyed," he reminded me.

My mother monitored me through dinner. "A quarter glass is plenty," she told me. "And make sure you have a few bites before you sip." Despite the parental hovering, I felt very grown up as I sipped my wine with my friends over dinner.

Over the next few years, my parents regularly allowed my brothers and I to have wine with our meals, and by the time I was sixteen, I was drinking a full glass with dinner. Upon going to the United States for college, I was amazed at the hoopla that surrounded turning eighteen, especially the way my peers all ran out to get totally sloshed. To me, drinking was simply a pleasurable addition to a meal, typically not a means to an end . . . and my European friends seemed to feel the same way. To this day, I drink very lightly and I never feel I "need" alcohol to have a good time. Maybe, I thought, an emphasis on moderation, along with early exposure guided by adults, is the key to responsible drinking.

There is no drinking age in Greece, or many other European countries. According to Alcoholics Anonymous, the United States has the highest rate of alcoholism in the world and almost three times the rate of Europe.

# OUTBACK COMPASSION

MY FRIEND JOHN, an athletic and adventurous hiker, decided to go Down Under for his vacation and explore the Australian outback. He flew into Sydney and connected north to Darwin, then picked up an outback tour to Alice Springs. En route the group made stops at Kakadu National Park, where John was awed by aboriginal rock paintings, and the site of Devil's Marbles, where huge, round, rust-colored granite rocks towered over the individuals in the group. The tour included six Americans and their guide, Wendy, a strapping twenty-six-year-old from Perth. Wendy energetically led the group on hikes. In the evenings, the cohort relaxed around a campfire. By day four, they had settled into a comfortable routine. After a hearty dinner of grilled kangaroo and emu, the low-key group stretched out around the fire and gazed at the moon lighting up the barren, dusty terrain.

John, who found himself sitting next to Wendy, asked her about her family. Wendy's eyes blinked and her usually can-do exterior softened.

"I lost my mother two months ago," she said, "cancer."

"I'm sorry," John whispered.

Wendy stared into the fire and absently poked at the logs with a twig. Wendy detailed her mother's ordeal. "She was in so much pain, it was unbearable to watch," she recalled. "She wasn't really living anymore, so we honored her request and called the doctor. We all said our good-byes and sent her on her way."

"You 'sent' her?" John asked in a hushed tone.

Wendy explained that, in cases of terminal illness, euthanasia is quietly condoned in the outback.

When John told me this story, I thought about my own father who had passed away the year before. My father had congestive heart failure and I had witnessed his slow, difficult physical decline. Finally, he had a stroke and after a week of lying in bed, gasping for breath, he died. His final, painful week was the most difficult of my life and left our family traumatized. It wasn't just the fact of his passing that was so excruciating; it was how deeply he suffered and how helpless we felt.

I remember rocking in the chair by his bedside, pleading with God to take him now and end his suffering. Even if euthanasia had been legal in the United States, could I have made the decision to end his life? I cannot honestly say. I was so distraught at the time that I don't know if I was in the proper state of mind to make such a momentous decision. Nor do I know what means could be used that would guarantee no pain. What I do know is that dying does not scare me, only the potential suffering that precedes it. I remember wondering at the time: if we put our animals out of their misery when they are in severe pain and there is no hope for recovery, why not the family members we love?

> The Northern Territories of Australia legalized doctor-sanctioned euthanasia in July 1996. Although the law was overturned on the federal level the following year due to a lobbying effort by opponents, doctor-assisted euthanasia is still discreetly practiced in the Northern Territories.

# FATEFUL GETAWAY

ROCHELLE, A FLIGHT attendant friend called me. "We have the same schedule next month," she sang. "Ten days off in the middle of the month. Arree-va-derchee Roma," she yelled.

"You're on!" I said.

The weather was perfect that week in mid-October, with sunny days and just a slight nip in the air at night. Rochelle, an attractive, leggy African American woman and I paraded through the Piazza Navonna on our way to Trevi Fountain. Along the way we found an outdoor café where we feasted on a lightly basted fried calamari appetizer and delicious grilled fish with fresh lemon, basil, and garlic.

I had some shopping to do and Rochelle wanted to sip her latte and people-watch, so I took off, agreeing to meet Rochelle in thirty minutes. A half an hour later, as I walked back toward the cafe, I could hear Rochelle's characteristic high-pitched giggle. At her feet, down on one knee with his arms dramatically outstretched, a well-dressed gentleman was crooning "Bellisima, bellisima." Then, as others gathered around, he started to serenade her, clutching his hands to his chest while Rochelle laughed and said, "I love this place."

"You are her friend, no?" asked Rochelle's admirer.

"Yes, we are friends," I assured him. He threw his open hands in the air, saying "grazie, grazie."

"I have dreamed about this woman," he told me dramatically. "I want to take her to dinner tonight." I looked at Rochelle; she coyly shrugged.

"By all means," I said. They made plans to meet that evening and before departing, he sang Rochelle another farewell ballad.

Delighted for Rochelle and content on my own, I toured the city that evening solo. As I walked past the Vatican, I recalled a conversation from the previous week, in which, Rochelle confessed to me that she had given up on finding love. She told me how, in the past decade, she had been on scores of blind dates, joined a dating service and even tried personal ads, but still hadn't found true love.

As the lock to the hotel room turned, I looked at the clock. It was three AM. I reached over and turned on the bedside lamp. Rochelle had tears running down her cheeks. I leaped out of bed and headed across the small room toward her.

"I finally found him," she stammered. "He's the one." I hugged and rocked her as her tears soaked my shoulder.

The next morning, while Rochelle reconnected with her new love, I peacefully sat in a small café and reflected on life. I wondered if, after a long search, Rochelle had really found her soul mate. And if that kind of synergy between two people really exists, I wondered how many potential soul mates we have in the world? Furthermore, if those soul mates live in other countries, how do we overcome those geographical obstacles in order to fulfill our romantic destinies?

> Love may find you when you least expect it.

# NATIVE KNOW-HOW

I WAS READY for a domestic vacation and a dose of camaraderie. I accepted an invitation to join a diverse group of fifteen flight attendants—straight, gay, men, women, old, young—on a houseboat cruising around Lake Powell in Utah for a week. The lake was both beautiful and strange with red clay hills periodically surfacing out of the water. Once we learned how to steer, dock the boat, and master the seemingly biggest challenge, emptying the commode, we enjoyed a relaxing week with a lot of laughs.

On our last day, we piled into four vans for our drive back to Phoenix and our flight to the east coast the following morning. On the way, we passed a Native American outpost in a remote town outside Mesa with a sign that said "visitors welcome." We walked in and met a chubby, genial guide named Andy. Before showing us the grounds, he gave us some background on the American Indian perspective on life.

He told us that for many Native Americans, life is conceptualized as a series of circles. The circle, he told us, is the symbol for reciprocal relationships. "You, me, and every other individual in the world is a dot in the center of our own circle," he explained. The first circle around that dot is divided into colored quadrants, with brown, yellow, white, and black representing the four races. A larger circle surrounding the innermost circle represents all of the animals. A third, even larger ecological circle, represents all plants and wildlife. Andy explained that it is each individual's responsibility to treat each person, animal, and living organism with respect.

I quietly stayed in the back of the pack and thought about Andy's explanation. The philosophy is simple, yet *so* powerful.

As we walked through the grounds, I looked at the cacti we passed and the golden retriever that was tagging along with our group with new appreciation. Andy pointed out interesting Indian artifacts, like thickly textured rugs, handmade baskets, and turquoise jewelry.

As we strolled along, Andy unexpectedly asked two of the men in our group if they were together.

"Well, yes, we are," one of them stammered.

"Don't be nervous," Andy smiled. "It's a good thing. You are gifted." Andy explained that in many American Indian cultures, gay members are revered and recognized for their ability to relate to both sexes and facilitate communication within the group.

> *Out of the Indian approach to life, there came an absorbing respect for life and principles of trust, honesty, generosity, equity, and brotherhood.*
> —Luther Standing Bear (1868–1937), Sioux Indian

# GAY SOLDIER

JEANINE AND I were looking for a quick, easy, cheap getaway. "How about London?" Jeanine suggested. "We can stay with my brother and his partner." With free airfare, a place to stay, and a six-hour flight from the east coast—about the same amount of time as getting to California—we agreed that it was a plan.

When Jeanine's brother, Jeremy, met us at Gatwick airport, he apologized that his partner Frank could not make it. "He's on maneuvers and will be home tonight," Jeremy said. That afternoon, Jeanine, Jeremy, and I went to Brighton and had fish and chips at a cottage inn beside the sea. Shortly after returning to the house just outside London, we met Frank. Frank, sporting a short military haircut, wore a sharply creased blue gray RAF uniform with a number of insignias and medals. He shook our hands warmly and gave Frank a kiss on the cheek.

That night, as the four of us sat in the kitchen noshing on shepherd's pie, I asked. "Is it difficult to be gay and in the military?"

Frank explained that his sexuality is a nonissue for him and thankfully, a nonissue for the British military. "I don't understand what the concern is in the U.S.," he said. "If women and men coexist in the military, why not gay men and straight men, or gay women and straight women?" He reached out and took Jeremy's hand. "We've been together for eight years," he said, "and I am not interested in anybody else." They squeezed each other's hand.

"Besides," Frank went on, "even if I was, what are straight men afraid of—that I will attack them?" We all laughed. "Are all straight men attracted to every woman they meet?" he asked. "I think not. So what makes straight men think I would be automatically attracted to them?"

Jeanine and I continued to discuss the issue on the flight home. "Although I'm straight, if someone of the same sex made a pass at me, I would simply say that I'm flattered but not interested," Jeanine said. "It's just not a big deal," she added.

I thought to myself: *yet it is a big deal to the powers-that-be in the U.S. military. What deeper fears lie behind our gay-unfriendly policies?*

Canada, Israel, England, and Holland allow gays to serve openly in their armed services.

# FRENCH AFFAIRS

IN PARIS FOR a few days, I called Lily and Maurice, a couple I knew who'd been married for many years. I'd met them several years ago while we were all on vacation touring the south of France and we'd kept in touch. Though Lily was out of town visiting her mother for the week, Maurice seemed delighted to hear from me and we agreed to meet for dinner. Over cocktails, Maurice, a still-handsome man with his unruly hair graying at the temples, pulled out his cell phone and made a call. I heard him making arrangements to meet at a local café in an hour.

"Who are we meeting?" I asked casually.

"You'll see Bill," Maurice said, beaming. "It will be fun," he assured me.

At the café, two women joined us and before long, Maurice had begun to outwardly flirt with one of the women. Within the hour, they were holding hands and nuzzling in a corner of the café, oblivious to their surroundings. Twisting in my seat, I finally tapped Maurice on the shoulder and asked him if I could talk to him for a moment. Scowling, he turned back to his friend and kissed her hand before abruptly standing.

We walked down the hall and out of the ladies' hearing range. *"Qu'est-ce que se passé?"* he said, clearly aggravated.

"What is *this*?" I threw back at him. "I am friends with both you and Lily," I explained. "Your behavior is putting me in a very awkward situation."

Maurice nodded and his face softened. *"Les Américains,"* he said. Tersely, I asked Maurice to forget my nationality for a moment and just help me to understand. He explained that he and Lily have an agreement. They can occasionally take on lovers, but with certain rules. For example, they have to let the other one know, they never take a lover more than once a year, they never continue an affair for more than a month, and they practice safe sex.

There was a long lull. I was struggling to understand. "Bill," Maurice said, "please do not judge us. For many French, it is understood and accepted. Lily and I love each other dearly and we will always be together. We have a wonderful life and family together and that will never change. But for us, sex is pleasure. If we want to keep sex interesting, occasionally we play a bit."

As I walked back to my hotel that evening, I wondered whether human beings are really meant to be monogamous. If Americans had more permissive relationships, would more marriages and families stay happily together? Or were the French just kidding themselves? I truly wasn't sure.

When French President Francois Mitterrand died in January 1996, his wife, sons, and mistress walked together arm-in-arm behind the coffin and procession. The Heritage Foundation reports the U.S. divorce rate is more than twice that of France and a 2004 Gallup poll reports ninety-one percent of Americans oppose married people having an affair.

# CENTRAL AMERICAN PRIORITIES

MY SENSES WERE on fire. Rich greenery and towering shady trees surrounded me. Inhaling deeply, I could practically smell the chlorophyll. Rays of toasty sunshine warmed my face. The entire country of Costa Rica seemed like one enormous sunny arboretum.

I slept heavily in the crisp, clean air that surrounded my bungalow-like hotel and upon waking, took a leisurely stroll through the famed Manuel Antonio National Reserve, with huge, dense trees hovering above. The park led to wide, white beaches with mammoth jagged rocks haphazardly scattered about. It was another perfectly lazy day in an ecological paradise with no set agenda. Late that afternoon, I found myself in a café overlooking the beach, mesmerized by the rising tide and rapidly approaching water lines. As I silently nursed a soda with no particular thoughts, the perfectly proportioned orange fireball slipped toward the horizon and crept behind a hill, lighting up the sky with purple and orange hues.

"It's beautiful," remarked a man, almost inaudibly, two tables over.

"Yes, it is amazing," I murmured.

He sat transfixed, staring at the sun, black sunglasses hugging his temples and long hair pulled back in a ponytail. A can of diet soda rested on the thigh of his shredded jean shorts. As I watched the last of the sun dip behind the horizon, the shirtless, tanned man next to me stretched and slowly reached his hand out.

"Juan," he quietly said.

I shook his hand. "Bill," I replied. Several minutes went by as I followed the purple hues spreading across the sky to unknown places.

"Your English is very good," I finally remarked.

"Hopefully as good as my French, German, Italian, and Portuguese," he responded.

"Five languages," I said, "You have two up on me!" We both laughed. He turned and for the first time looked at me with a smile. He told me he taught school outside the capital, San José, and loved Costa Rica. I asked him to tell me something I should know about the country.

"If there is one thing you should know, it's that Costa Ricans are a peaceful, bright group. We have no military, education is stressed, and learning languages is a priority."

Juan left a few minutes later and I sat in silence, taking in the soothing vistas in front of me. *Nice priorities,* I thought to myself. *No war, lots of learning, and the ability to communicate with people of many cultures.* I took a deep breath, inhaling the salty air and peering across the sea.

I wondered: *If learning languages and getting international exposure are priorities for a relatively poor country like Costa Rica, why aren't they emphasized for countries like the United States?*

> According to a 2004 U.S. Department of Education survey, only one-third of American public secondary school students are enrolled in foreign-language classes.

# ISRAELI REFLECTION

MOSHE AND I met in college and have kept in touch over the last twenty years. He is a tall, muscular forty-two-year-old man with a head of tousled black curls. He is also a devout follower of Kabbala, a type of Judaism. As he proudly says, "I was a Kabbalist way before Madonna and Hollywood made it chic." Moshe lives in Tel Aviv with his wife, Ariel, and their two children, but often travels to Europe on business. Coincidentally, two years ago we both planned to be in Madrid at the same time in early December and made plans to meet for dinner.

When we met in the hotel lobby, we both grinned.

"You are getting old," he said with a chuckle.

Not missing a beat, I retorted "You look even older!" We laughed and slapped each other on the back. But my observation was true. Moshe had gray bags under his eyes and had noticeably aged since we'd seen each other two years earlier.

We went to a tapas restaurant where we sampled several small dishes of seafood, meats, and beans and ordered a carafe of the house Rioja wine. As we talked about our lives, I asked Moshe about his plans for the upcoming Passover. His genial smile disappeared: he became more intent and serious.

"Our lives are difficult," he said wringing his hands. "We are afraid of terrorism. I am afraid to go to the office, my wife is afraid to go shopping, my kids are afraid to go to school." His eyes began to moisten.

I leaned closer and said, "I can only imagine what it must be like."

He began to talk about something he'd been thinking about all day. "I want to regain my belief in humanity and I want that attitude to carry over to my family—and especially to my kids."

By the time the creamy rice pudding dessert arrived, Moshe was more relaxed. *"Muchas, muchas gracias,"* Moshe said to the smiling waitress. When we got up to leave, he approached the owner to shake his hand. Then he put his thumb and two index fingers together and brought them to his lips, saying *"Bueno, bueno."* Laughing, the owner responded *"Si, si, gracias."*

We slowly walked the long way back to the area that housed our hotels, past the Prado Museum and the Royal Palace, magnificently aglow in floodlights. "Being away from home and preparing for Passover has given me a chance to put some thoughts in perspective," Moshe said. He patted my shoulder and said, "There are many things I can't control. I can only control how I react to them. So I will live my life positively, role model behavior for my kids, and trust the power of destiny for the rest."

I walked Moshe to his hotel. As I headed to my own place for the evening, I wondered what it would be like to live Moshe's life. I shuddered. Could I handle the daily threat and fear of violence and political reprisals? I decided to only invest energy in what I can control. At that moment, I recommitted myself to living my day-to-day life in a respectful and loving way.

> In Israel, Kabbalists celebrate holidays by reflecting on their lives and ways in which they can gain balance between actions, emotions, mind, and spirit. Kabbalists create sacred space in honor of these holidays by taking off from their everyday life to work on themselves psychologically and spiritually.

# DANISH SPIRITUALITY

I LANDED IN Copenhagen on a Saturday morning and after a short nap, I called my friend Stefan to make plans for the next day. He suggested we meet at nine AM and enjoy the day in the city. Not wanting Stefan to alter his routine, I offered to meet later in case he had Sunday church plans. "No," he said. "No church here."

The next morning at the hotel I had a delicious full Scandinavian buffet breakfast that fueled me for the day—three soft boiled eggs, two slices of grainy wheat bread, a wedge of Gouda cheese, and a bowl of fiber-rich mueslix. I felt ready for a day of touring.

In front of the hotel, I met Stefan, a tall blond with a deep voice and an Adam's apple that bobs when he speaks. We walked across a small square toward a tiny harbor. Taking a small boat with several other tourists, we toured the canals in and around the city, passing the "Little Mermaid" statue, and gaining an interesting perspective on the narrow streets and worn buildings that make up this city, built on the waterway between Denmark and Sweden. After the boat tour, we cut through the city and strolled down the *Stroget* (translates into "made for strolling"), the longest pedestrian-only street in Europe.

Pointing at a small, bland corner café, Stefan said, "That was one of Soren Kierkegaard's favorite places."

"The famous existentialist," I responded, adding with a chuckle, "His philosophy wasn't particularly upbeat."

Stefan smiled. "Maybe Kierkegaard was just a realist," he said.

Copenhagen is pristine and quiet by day, but at night it comes alive with packed streets, neon-lit shops, and beer-guzzling nightclubs. Tivoli Gardens, a mini-Disneyworld in the middle of the city, combines the feel of an upscale amusement park with a flower-laden, well-groomed estate. En route to a free pantomime show in one of Tivoli's theaters, Stefan and I passed a merry-go-round of Viking ships, an Arabian Palace housing over twenty restaurants, and a beautiful lake with ducks and swans.

Waiting for the show to begin, I mentioned to Stefan that I didn't recall seeing any churches during our tour of Copenhagen. He said that churches exist but few Danes attend.

"So people practice their faith from home, I suppose," I asked.

"No," he shrugged. "We are not a religious group." As the show started, I watched an excellent comic performance by an actor wearing a large black derby hat and heavy, clownlike makeup. But, I couldn't help wondering about Stefan's comments. *Are most Danes atheists and if so, are they spiritual on any level?*

Walking toward the hotel after the show, we laughed and made small talk about some of the show's skits. Then I said, "I am still amazed by the Danish approach to religion."

He responded that many Danes are either atheists or agnostics—that is, they question the existence of God. "To me, the Bible seems like a story," he said. "An interesting one perhaps, but just a story. And a story that unfortunately is often taken out of context to support judgmental opinions of people."

"Like many Scandinavians, we live and let live. We do not intrude in others' lives. I think many organized religions are similar to cults, focusing on power and control. I simply trust my instincts to live my life the right way. So yes, I have a spiritual life, but I account to myself." I was speechless and my mind whirled. We walked in silence. Approaching the hotel, I smiled at Stefan and thanked him for an interesting day and went to my room.

Lying in bed that night, I couldn't sleep. I turned on the light and propped myself up in bed. *Does God exist or not? And if so, who's God?* Knowing the Danes have few homeless and little poverty, I wondered: *is the Danish societal norm, relying on simply doing the right thing, the most compassionate spiritual approach?*

> According to Scandinavian government statistics, over half of Norwegians, Swedes, and Danes say that God does not matter to them at all. Religious apathy is also apparent in other European countries. In the Netherlands, Britain, Germany, Sweden, and Denmark, fewer than one in ten people attend church once a month or more.

# 9
# Be My GUEST

# LEBANESE GIFT

KATIE, SIMON, HUDA, Muna, and I strolled arm-in-arm through downtown Beirut to the home of yet another family friend for Sunday lunch. Opening the door, an older, heavy-set woman smiled warmly and said, "I'm Juliette," as she engulfed me in a bear hug and kissed me once on each cheek.

"I'm Misho," the balding fifty-something man behind her said as he repeated the cheek-kissing ritual. In the next ten minutes, I met well over twenty strangers, each greeting me with a friendly double kiss. This was the second week of my visit to Beirut and I felt relaxed and in the groove, thoroughly enjoying the feeling of belonging. I found myself returning hugs and kissing everybody I met upon saying hello and good-bye.

After lunch, I went with Huda and Muna to Acrivie and Stepho's home, two very affectionate family friends who lived in bustling downtown Beirut. On the way to their home, Huda, Muna, and I paraded past designer-dressed Lebanese as they poured in and out of cafes, restaurants, and department stores on chic Hamra Street. Acrivie opened the door with her wide smile and blazing blue eyes. *"Ahlan, ahlan,"* she said welcoming us with double kisses. Instantly, I felt the warm hospitality swim over me.

Entering the expansive living room, I noticed a beautiful small painting mounted on the wall. After a delicious lunch, I went over and took in the watercolor of an outdoor bazaar.

"Do you like it?" Stepho asked me.

"It's amazing," I said, smiling in admiration.

Stepho removed the painting from the wall and gave it to me. "It's for you," he said smiling.

I was astounded. "Oh no, I couldn't," I stammered. "I was just commenting on how beautiful it is."

"Please," Stepho said. "It gives me pleasure to see you happy." I looked around the room at the smiling faces. Acrivie came up to me and kissed me on both cheeks.

"For you," she said. "A present to remember Lebanon." I was so overcome that I couldn't respond and graciously accepted the gift.

I now find myself giving away personal items that I know somebody else will cherish. A coworker was admiring a hand-carved aircraft in my office. Without thinking twice I gave it to him and saw his face light up. I had enjoyed the plane for several years, it was time to spread that pleasure. Try it; it feels great to share something special with others.

| It is better to give than to receive. |
|---|

# HAITIAN HURRAH

SEVERAL YEARS AGO, a friend told me about a group of airline employees who utilize their flying benefits to transport Third World children in need of medical care to the United States. *"I have a few days off,"* I said to myself. Before I knew it, I had volunteered. After filling out an application and going through a series of phone interviews, I found myself with an itinerary to Haiti.

I landed at chaotic Port-au-Prince airport and found the individual holding the sign with the organization's name on it. He introduced me to the family waiting nearby. We exchanged pleasantries. A few minutes later it was time to go and I will never forget the moment that two tearful Haitian parents handed me their four-year-old daughter. "Please," Monique's father pleaded through his bloodshot eyes. "Take care of my girl," he said softly, his voice breaking.

"In my heart, I know she will be fine," I said in my best French as I stroked Monique's cleft lip while my own bottom lip quivered. Her mother began to wail and she buried her head in her husband's shoulder as I turned and awkwardly holding the bewildered little girl's hand, headed toward the gate. Two weeks later, I saw those same faces when I brought their daughter home; however, this time the tears were of happiness. With Monique's surgery a success, her mother held her daughter and rocked her while Monique's father put his arms around both of them. *"Merci, merci bien,"* Monique's father said as he motioned me to join the family. Putting his arm around me, he gently brushed the tears from my cheeks as we all rocked together.

Random acts of hospitality may improve your health. David McClelland, a psychologist from Harvard University, reports a link between selfless acts of kindness and a stronger immune system.

# BALI HIGH

WHEN MARK TALKS about his vacation to Bali, his eyes take on a faraway look. "It's not just the physical beauty of the flowers or the temples or the beaches." He told me. "It's the magic in the soul of the people."

Mark recalled his first day on the island. After a short nap at the hotel, he left his resort for a walk. Throughout the small town, he heard dancing flutes and light, soothing bongo taps emanating from a temple. The sounds had a calming effect and he felt as though he was swaying together with the locals as he made his way through the streets of the village.

At one point, he stopped at a store to get a bottle of sunscreen. When Mark was checking out, the smiling clerk noticed the bottle was chipped and insisted on getting Mark another bottle. Then, the clerk profusely thanked Mark for visiting his store and escorted him out the door as a host would do for a guest.

Seeing a sign for a massage, Mark stopped in. After inquiring about the price—seven dollars for an hour!—he decided to indulge. After losing himself in the superb massage, Mark realized that the massage was twenty minutes over the agreed upon hour. The masseuse explained that Mark seemed so relaxed that she decided to continue. When Mark offered the masseuse a five-dollar tip, she looked embarrassed and confused. He realized she had extended the time because she knew it would make him happy, not for financial gain.

On the way home, Mark felt relaxed and nurtured. When he stopped for a bottle of water from a refreshment stand, he received a cool eucalyptus towel with his drink. The concessionaire smiled and handed the towel to Mark with a slight bow.

"Thank you," she said.

"No, thank you!" Mark replied.

Mark realized that the Hindus in Bali do nice things for others simply because they want to see other people happy. Mark told me how he incorporated his experience into his own life. He found himself looking for ways to help others—holding doors open for strangers, helping a mother carry her groceries to her car, and running errands for an elderly neighbor. "The fact is I got more out of it than I put into it," Mark said. "Small acts of kindness are what connect us as people."

> It is the small, insignificant, simple gestures that make life bearable. A smile, a touch, a word, a kindness, a concern.

# GUAM HOSPITALITY

GINA, A FRIEND who now lives in Texas, loved growing up on the island of Guam. She is Chamoru, a multiethnic culture unique to Guam. Guam was discovered by the Spanish, occupied by the Japanese and liberated by the United States in 1944. Gina is a striking woman, with a slight Asian tilt to her wide eyes and full European lips. I asked her about her fondest memory growing up in Guam. "Fiesta," Gina said without hesitation. "Fiestas are the best and most unique part of Guam."

At least every month, a different town sponsors a "Village Fiesta"—a huge party that celebrates a patron saint with open houses that feature bars, bands, and an abundance of food. Big tents are erected by each family in the yards surrounding the Spanish-shingled cement homes. Rows of folding chairs and benches line the yard. Nobody needs an invitation—it is just a big welcoming celebration that takes place on practically every Sunday afternoon somewhere on the island and continues well into the evening. You can sing along with karaoke, dance the cha-cha, and have fun. Simply turn, greet the person next to you with a kiss on the cheek and mingle! Then, make your way through the buffet line and even as the festivities wind down, graciously accept a plate of food to take home with you.

A local favorite was called *kelaguen*. The main ingredients—either chicken, beef, or shrimp—are marinated in soy sauce and sautéed with grated coconut, onions, hot peppers, and lemon juice and served over red rice (which is actually Japanese orange sticky rice). Grab a paper plate and enjoy the picnic!

Gina laughed as she told me how she provided directions to friends planning on that weekend's fiesta. "Take a right at the second white house and a left at the speed bump. Once you pass the second line of trees, take another left." There are no street names in Guam; it's just a series of winding roads that are second nature to the locals. But, as Gina reiterated, it's worth the effort. "It's a wonderful chance for us to bond as a community," Gina said. "It's always a chance to reconnect with old friends and meet new ones."

A traveler walking wearily into a remote village and greeted by smiles finds that village home.

# BULL RUN

MIGUEL, A SPANISH friend whom I met on vacation in Greece, invited me to visit him in his hometown of Pamplona. "Come for the annual 'running of the bulls,'" he said. "It is very fun!"

After I arrived, Miguel showed me around the small city and told me about the upcoming celebration that would begin two days later. I was shocked to find out that the entire run of the bulls only takes about three minutes!

On the day of the big event, we got up with the sunrise and walked to the Santo Domingo corral, on the outskirts of the city, where we saw a number of bulls in a fenced-in area. "Six of them are wild bulls," explained Miguel, "and the rest of them are tame." Miguel explained that the wild ones rev up the others in the pack, which makes for an exciting run. Nervously, I turned to Miguel and explained that although I would like to see the spectacle, I had no intention of getting in the way. "Me either!" laughed Miguel. Although many find running in front of the bulls thrilling, I was relieved Miguel did not expect me to participate. "But we'll find a good spot to watch!" I said.

We walked back to the center of town where a group was

starting to congregate. "Here comes the blessing," Miguel said. The group broke into a song that Miguel translated for me. "We ask San Fermin, as our patron, to guide us through the bull run and give us his blessing." I shuddered as I thought about the bulls charging down the street.

"I hope San Fermin comes through," I said.

At exactly eight AM, I heard a "crack," like a gun firing, that made me flinch and duck.

"Bill," Miguel chided laughing. "Try to relax." Miguel told me that the first sound indicates that the bulls are starting to move. Shortly thereafter, another crack sounded. I looked expectantly at Miguel. "All the bulls are out of the corral," he explained, as we leaned forward against the wall, waiting for the onslaught. As crowds of people ran in front of us, we could hear screams of laughter. Just a couple of feet behind them were the first group of bulls chasing them. Two teenagers jumped up on our wall as the bulls raced by them. Both young men fell back between Miguel and I, laughing and patting each other on the back. Then, suddenly, the race was over.

"Is that it?" I asked Miguel.

"Yes," he said. "Takes only three minutes!"

A third "crack" went off and I looked at Miguel. "The bulls are in the ring," he interpreted. Not even a minute later, a fourth crack went off.

"Okay, now what?" I asked. Miguel laughed. "That means it's really over—and I promise you that's the last crack!"

The annual Running of the Bulls in Pamplona, Spain, started in 1591, meeting the need to move bulls from the countryside to the arena. Locals began running in front of the animals in the 1600s. The event was made famous by Ernest Hemingway's 1927 novel, *The Sun Also Rises.*

# SEVILLE SIESTA

BEFORE GOING TO Seville, my friend Edgar and I made a day of it in Madrid with a quick visit to the Prado Museum and a few favorite stores near the Plaza Mayor. Then Edgar and I hopped on the comfortable AVE train for the three-hour ride to Seville. Arriving in the early evening, we found a quaint bed and breakfast housed in a large nine-bedroom villa. The splendid home featured stained glass windows, large Oriental rugs, elaborate chandeliers, and multiple wrought-iron balconies, which overlooked several orange trees in the gardens. Edgar, who speaks Spanish, asked the owner of the B & B for a meal recommendation and was given directions to the owner's favorite restaurant. Edgar wrote down the directions in English so we could both navigate our way: walk to the left, the road will somewhat curve to the right, then take the third fork in the road to the left and follow that road as it winds down toward the town.

Edgar and I looked at each other. *"Bueno,"* Edgar said to the owner with a smile.

As we left the inn, I murmured to Edgar, "If we see a sign that says 'Welcome to Portugal,' I think we can safely assume we took the wrong turn." Chuckling, we went in search of the restaurant.

Eventually, we found the secluded eatery, which was packed with local patrons. We had a delicious meal of roast pig and paella "al fresco" on an exquisite flower-laden patio with purple flowers growing like ivy up the surrounding walls. It took us two hours to find our way back to the inn after dinner, but the wandering journey was an unforgettable experience. Although we were "lost" among the maze of alley streets, a few large avenues served as markers that oriented and guided us. We stared in amazement at the charming architecture, which included golden-hued villas with castle-like features, lit up by subtle lighting. We strolled along the Guadalquivir River through the park and past the monuments and churches that lined the waterway. Looking directly across the river and the sight of charming Seville, we enjoyed a panoramic view of the lit-up city, church steeples aglow alongside ancient clocks and arched domes.

The next morning we slept in. After a leisurely breakfast, we started to tour the city full of energy and enthusiasm. But after a relatively short time, store windows began to slam shut and doors were locked. Within a thirty-minute time span, the city metamorphosed from a busy, crowded metropolis to a ghost town, without a soul in sight.

"What happened?" I asked Edgar, astonished. "Is it a holiday?"

Edgar shook his head. "Siesta time," he explained. "Nothing will open again until five."

"When in Seville, do as the Spaniards do," I joked, "nap!" It was wonderful. I escaped the intense heat of midday and awoke refreshed each evening, ready to enjoy the night life of Seville. I took a nap every day on that weeklong trip and returned to the U.S. feeling relaxed and well rested. I now try to incorporate a nap into my daily life, time permitting!

According to sleep researcher James McKenna, humans are "biphasic sleepers," that is, we are designed to sleep twice in a twenty-four-hour period.

# HULA BIRTHDAY

IT WAS MY longest birthday ever. I was flying to Maui from the East Coast of the U.S. with six friends and chasing the sun. The flight from L.A. had just a handful of passengers and before long, the crew found out it was my birthday. We had a festive and playful celebration, including a game of tag that had us darting between rows of seats at 35,000 feet and compressing each other into overhead bins.

However, the best part of our one-week vacation was yet to come. Our hotel was the very last one on Kaanapali Beach and splendidly quiet with few people and only the sounds of crashing waves. Mesmerized by the Pacific vistas, we circumvented towering mountains that peeked over turquoise ripples as we wound our way toward Hana. Upon arriving, we headed straight for the torrential waterfalls and flung ourselves under the barrage of water. The seven of us laughed until our stomachs hurt as our knees buckled under the force of the natural shower. On the third night of the trip, at three AM, we drove to Haleakala, the inactive volcano, and looked at the ash- and lava-covered combs from atop the crater. It felt as though we were on the moon. Then, as the sun rose, we stared in awe at the pink and amber hues reflecting off the rocks. Later, we hopped on bikes and cycled back down to the main town for a seven AM breakfast.

On the second half of our trip, we slowed down a bit and got to know each other better. We were seven close friends relaxing together: sleeping in, taking long walks on the beach, climbing into a hammock for a nap, talking about life and dreams. We were three men, four women, some gay, some straight, some Caucasian, some Asian, and some African American, and it was refreshing to experience that none of these external differences mattered. The feelings of being close and authentic and the lack of pressure to entertain each other made for one of the most relaxing, bonding, and rewarding vacations I have ever enjoyed. And the vacation was certainly one of the most memorable birthdays I've ever experienced. I now spend my birthday commemorating that special time, celebrating friends who come naturally and comfortably, and setting some time aside to reflect on magical experiences. *Mahalo!*

> *There are persons so radiant, so genial, so kind, so pleasure-bearing, that you instinctively feel, in their presence, that they do you good.*
>
> —Henry Ward Beecher (1813–1887)

# POLISH KARMA

TRACY WAS HAVING a fabulous time exploring the beautiful city of Krakow. The majestic buildings, set off by stone architecture and indoor marble accents, gave the city a formal, regal feel. *"One of Europe's best-kept secrets,"* she thought to herself. Although she hadn't planned on doing anything somber on vacation, she decided to set aside a day to visit nearby Auschwitz. *"When am I ever going to be this close to it again?"* she asked herself.

The day was disturbing. She traced the steps of those who made their way into the lethal showers and shuddered. Her mind reeling, Tracy boarded the wrong train on her way back to Krakow. It was getting dark. Tracy asked for help, but nobody spoke English as the train sped into the countryside. When nothing looked familiar, Tracy started to panic. She realized that with every minute, she was moving farther away from Krakow. Then, at the next station, a young man got on the train. "Please tell me you speak some English," Tracy pleaded. The young man winced and put his index finger toward his thumb in front of his face.

"Kraakkoow," Tracy said. The teen shook his head, indicating she was on the wrong train. Then, he held up his hand indicating she should wait. When the train stopped, he motioned her to follow him. He got off with her at the next stop, walked her to the ticket counter to buy another ticket, and then showed her the track while pointing at the sign indicating the departure time. Tracy smiled and nodded several times and said over and over again, "thank you, thank you." The young man smiled, waved, and made his way to the track across the way.

Tracy eyes softened and began to tear. She boarded her train and went to the window to look out at her helper. As their eyes met, they waved to each other. She felt even more grateful when she noted the departure time of the young man's train. His train to continue his journey wasn't leaving for another three hours.

Upon arriving back in the U.S., Tracy was running through JFK airport in New York City trying to catch a connecting flight to Philadelphia when she noticed a young woman standing alone. The girl, who might have been twenty, was looking around tearfully. She looked scared and confused. Tracy stopped and smiled. "Can I help you?" she asked slowly. The girl smiled nervously and pulled out a piece of paper with a Brooklyn address on it. Tracy motioned for the young girl to follow her and walked her through the crowd toward the taxi stand. Helping the girl into the cab, Tracy and her new friend exchanged waves as the cab pulled away from the curb. Tracy smiled and shrugged. *"I'll catch the next flight,"* she thought to herself.

| |
|---|
| All people smile in the same language. |

# NAIROBI NICETIES

BY THE TIME I landed in Nairobi, I was dehydrated and exhausted. As if the transatlantic flight wasn't draining enough, my connecting flight from London to Nairobi had a six-hour mechanical delay. After finally arriving at my downtown hotel near the Kenyatta Conference Center, I collapsed into bed. Several hours later, I awoke with a start. "*What time is it?*" I wondered. Then I panicked. "*What* day *is it?*" I had been traveling for days and was completely disoriented. My heart started to race. *Had I missed my safari tour to South Nairobi National Park?*

I leaped out of bed and rummaged through my bag for some clothes. Dressing quickly in a T-shirt and jeans, I bypassed the elevator and ran down the stairs, two at a time, heading toward the front desk. Five feet from the desk, I blurted out, "What time and day is it?" The attractive, luminous-faced woman behind the counter with the name "Annetta" pinned on her lapel stared back at me silently. Wondering if she understood me and still gasping for breath, I repeated, "Time? Day?"

She smiled. "I understand you," she responded softly with an impeccable British accent. "It's four in the morning and I can assure you that if you planned to do something yesterday, you have missed it. And if you plan to do something today, you have the ability to be on time." Initially, I couldn't decide if she was being condescending or concerned. But then, her smile broadened and softened her face, revealing two rows of perfect teeth.

"Well . . . thank you," I stammered. She gave me the tour information that I needed and then explained that haste is the greatest sign of disrespect in Africa.

"Go slowly," she advised. "And," she added, "in Africa, it is important to always greet others before conducting business."

"Now, let's start over the proper way," she said playfully. "Good morning," she said, as she cocked her head to the side and leaned toward me. She slowly asked "How are you?" followed by a gracious "Are you enjoying your stay?" I felt myself relax and take on her calm demeanor. Our eyes locked and I sensed her sincerity.

"Annetta," she said, holding out her hand.

"Bill," I responded taking her hand with a smile and feeling my heartbeat return to normal.

"I am so glad you elected to visit our country," she said.

"No Annetta, I am so glad I elected to visit your country and have the opportunity to meet people like you," I said. "You reminded me to be polite and gracious—no matter what the situation."

*One who greets another, profits by it; one who does not, loses by it.*
—African proverb

# TURKISH TWIST

ON MY SECOND day in Istanbul, I made my way to the Grand Bazaar, the largest covered market in the world, where native merchants offer carpets, jewelry, brass, leather, and spices. Although I did not intend to shop, I spotted an Oriental rug with a unique gold and terra cotta design that I decided would look great in my office at home. Having read a bit about the art of bargaining, I ventured into turf I found unnerving. *"Why don't they just put a price on it and let it go at that?"* I thought to myself.

I smiled uneasily at the swarthy, mustached salesman, who smiled back. "How much?" I asked, pointing to the rug.

"For you, my friend," he replied, "two hundred dollars." I was prepared to bargain in lira, but was relieved that the salesman wanted dollars.

"Fifty," I firmly said, surprising myself with my boldly low offer.

Not flinching, the salesman replied, "One hundred eighty." We stared at each other; I was afraid that looking away would signal weakness.

"Seventy," I said evenly, dropping my smile and going for a

poker-faced look. I really wanted the rug and probably would have paid the full price, but I found myself enjoying this new endeavor. Still smiling, the merchant rocked his head back and forth.

"One hundred fifty," he said. He looked as though he was enjoying this too. I couldn't help but smile back.

"Ninety," I retorted, wondering where this was going to end. He bit down on his lower lip and stared at me intently, dropping his smile.

"Eighty," he said firmly.

"Huh?" I responded. The salesman threw his head back and roared. I, too, started laughing as he walked toward me and wrapped me up in a hug. Introducing himself as Anwar, he put his arm around my shoulders and brought me inside his small, cramped shop where his wife served me tea. Anwar told me that his son was in college in the U.S. "He will be an engineer," he said with pride. Anwar wanted to know about life in America, if I had ever been to Houston where his son is, and what the city is like. When I left, he insisted that I take the rug for eighty dollars.

"Special price for a friend," he said, smiling warmly.

> According to Shop Around the World.com, shoppers in Turkey will get the best deal when they have a personal relationship with the merchant. If the shopkeeper likes you, you can expect to get a good price.

# GHANA GALA

"LET'S GO TO the airline party tonight," said Patrick, a flight attendant friend in his early forties, with whom I regularly play racquetball. In celebration of the New Year, he told me, there would be door prizes for free tickets to cities around the world. When we arrived, the event was in full swing. Door prizes had already been given for free trips to Hong Kong, Paris, Athens, and Rio. An hour later, the next series of number were called. Patrick jumped out of his chair. "That's me, I won!"

Patrick returned to the table, looking deflated. "A free round-trip to Ghana," he said. "Yaaaay," he added sarcastically.

"I think it sounds great, Patrick," I encouraged him. "What an opportunity." Gradually, he warmed to the prize, and the following month Patrick announced that he planned to use his free trip—with conditions.

"I plan on a week, but I reserve the right to make it just a long weekend," he made clear. Two weeks after his departure, Patrick still had not returned to the U.S. Many of us started to wonder if he was ever coming home.

Arriving in Accra, the bustling English-speaking capital of

Ghana, Patrick was instantly welcomed. He told me that as he walked to the taxi from the airport, two children yelled out *"obruni"* and waved. Not knowing what that meant, he smiled and waved back. Arriving at the hotel, he got out of the taxi and once again, a child called out *"obruni."* Turning around, he spotted the child's smile and exchanged waves.

Upon checking into the modern, fifteen-dollar-per-night hotel, Patrick met Winston, the jovial, crisply attired, twenty-something clerk behind the desk. Patrick asked him about the meaning of *"obruni"* and Winston chuckled.

"'*Obruni*' literally means foreigner," he said in his clipped British dialect. "The children are welcoming you to Ghana." When Winston invited Patrick to his home for dinner that evening with his family, Patrick eagerly accepted.

One of about twelve guests invited to Winston's family home for dinner that evening, Patrick felt honored to be part of the group. Nobody in Winston's family knew about Patrick's arrival until he knocked on the door, but nobody seemed concerned. Winston's parents and two sisters had also invited unannounced friends, so it appeared to be a spontaneous get-together. Although none of the guests knew each other, everyone mingled easily. There were two British couples, a Ghanaian family of five, two Canadian girls, and Patrick.

"How does your family know how much food to prepare?" Patrick asked Winston.

"We always have enough for an army," he replied. "Our

family loves to entertain and meet new people. This is just another night at our house."

Eating at a leisurely pace, Patrick listened as his hosts discussed their culture. He learned that in Ghana, a successful person is not measured by economic wealth, but rather by how well he or she treats others. One visitor added, "Material goods are to be shared with others. Selfishness belongs to the witches and sorcerers."

As Patrick enjoyed *fufu,* a pounded soft taro root that is very tasty and filling, his admiration for his Ghanian hosts continued to grow. "You are the friendliest people I have ever met," he exclaimed.

"Of course," Winston said. "We may be saving ourselves!" The Ghanaians roared while the foreigners looked baffled. Patrick learned that Ghanaians believe that their ancestors return to earth as "pale-skinned" people to test the hospitality of their children, so it is important to treat foreigners well and to instill hospitality in your kids.

"So you might be my father!" one of the Ghanaian guests remarked, motioning to Patrick. The whole room cracked up, but there was a serious undertone to the discussion. Friendliness toward visitors is a focal point of the culture.

As Patrick relayed his experience, I wondered how my U.S. friends and relatives would respond to this attitude of welcome. We are so cautious and suspicious in the United States—and especially wary of strangers.

Is there a way I can instill in them the belief in humanity, a sense of hospitality, and the welcoming friendliness Patrick experienced in Ghana without encouraging them to put themselves in a potentially dangerous situation?

> *I am because we are.*
> —African proverb

# GOOD ON YA, MATE!

SEVERAL YEARS AGO, I toured Australia with Chris, an airline buddy. After a long flight halfway around the world and a short nap at our hotel, Chris suggested that we find a bar and celebrate our arrival with a beer.

"Sounds good to me," I laughed. "I don't know what time it is here, but it has to be happy hour somewhere in the world. Besides, the sun is starting to set, so maybe we can get on the local time zone."

Exiting the hotel, we found ourselves looking straight ahead at the Opera House, a modern, New Age looking structure that overlooks the city of Sydney and the waterway. Behind the Opera House was a huge bridge that connected various parts of the city with visible beaches built into the coastline.

"Amazing," Chris said as we took in the bustling city and looked at the restaurants and cafes lining the waterway.

I pointed toward a friendly-looking bar and said, "Let's go!"

Chris and I shuffled through the crowded room and made our way to the bar. Standing in front of a line of taps, I said to the bartender, "Two beers please."

"Two pints for the Yanks," said the blond, ruddy-cheeked bartender, tossing the mugs in the air.

Suddenly the two girls next to me squealed, "Oh, Americans! Say something!"

Laughing, I stammered, "I don't know what to say!"

Both girls screamed again and turned to Chris. "Go on, say something, anything, just talk!" Chris looked at me. I shrugged.

"Why?" Chris asked, turning his palms skyward.

The girls screamed again and hugged us. The girl hanging on Chris exclaimed, "We love Americans, everything about you!"

Now that's what I call a warm welcome.

| It isn't always what you say, it's how you say it. |
|---|

# TOMATO TOSS

CRAIG, A SPANISH-speaking friend, was touring Spain in August with his girlfriend, Jody. He was in Valencia when he heard about *"La Tomantina"* from the front desk clerk at the hotel.

"It's a fight with tomatoes," he translated to Jody. They exchanged looks.

"Craig," she said rolling her eyes, "maybe you should ask her again."

Craig once again engaged the hotel clerk. "Yup," Craig said. "It's a huge food fight in the nearby town of Bunol. It happens every year at this time, when there is a surplus of tomatoes after the harvest." They looked at each other and smiled.

"We're there!" Jody said.

Early the next morning, the couple drove to Bunol. Although the festival didn't start until eleven AM, the small town was mobbed by nine and the couple had to park outside the town and walk to the event. As they passed several small homes and shops in the city, they noticed that all of the windows were covered in protective tarps. Music played everywhere, and the couple joined a group outside one of the bars for a beer. At eleven AM, several huge dump trucks filled with surplus tomatoes pulled into one of the main square. All at once, they dumped their tomatoes onto the grass. Immediately, people scooped up the ripe red fruit and started hurling it at each other.

Within seconds, Jody was hit on the side of her head. She turned to see who threw it and got a second smack right in her mouth. Laughing, she returned the volley. Within minutes, both Jody and Craig were covered. The narrow streets of the town had become red rivers. Craig lay down in a "tomato pond" and roared with laughter. He was completely immersed except for his head.

Afterward, he told Jody, "Two hours of constant aggression was such a relief for me—it rid me of my hostilities for a year!"

In 2004, *La Tomantina* attracted over 36,000 participants, who pelted each other with over 140 tons of tomatoes.

# CZECH CHUCK

KAREL, A CZECH friend, whom I was visiting in Poland, was making plans to visit her hometown of Prague.

"Join me!" she invited me. "You will love Czechoslovakia and I have someplace special to take you," she said with a smile. When we arrived and hopped into a cab, I heard Karel say something to the driver about the Café Imperial. As we sat in the backseat, Karel wore a mischievous grin.

"Okay, what is it about this place?" I asked.

"Nothing," Karel said with a laugh. She tapped my knee. "Let's just have fun," she said.

Walking into the café, I stopped at the doorway just to take it in. The ceilings and walls were tiled with colorful ceramics that offset marble pillars and inlaid columns. A tuxedo-clad waiter led us to our table. I ordered a steak and Karel mentioned something to the waiter about a Saturnin's Bowl. The waiter smiled conspiratorially. He returned with a large metal bowl and set it in front of Karel. The bowl contained a heaping mound of jelly doughnuts. I stared at Karel, bewildered.

"What did you order?" I asked.

Without a word, Karel picked up one of the doughnuts and smashed it against my face, exploding into hysterics.

Jumping up and wiping the jelly from my mouth, I exclaimed, "What is wrong with you?"

Karel stood up, picked up another doughnut and winged it through the air. I turned my head and it clipped my ear. Laughter exploded from all corners of the café, and doughnuts started flying from the table next to us.

Still unsure about what was transpiring, I instinctively ducked under our table and hid for about a minute. Then, getting my bearings, I got up, grabbed a doughnut, and heaved it straight at Karel, catching her right in the forehead. After all the doughnuts were gone, we hugged and laughed until our sides hurt. Then we joined the folks at the table next to us for some real dessert!

The Imperial Café keeps a huge supply of stale doughnuts on hand. Food fights are an advertised form of celebration for birthdays, graduations, and evidently, out-of-town guests!

# KOREAN CARING

LAURA AND LEIGH, two longtime friends of mine, are identical twins in their late thirties. Both are single, and avid travelers with a contagious zest for life. They were in the midst of a monthlong tour through the Far East when the tragedies of September eleventh struck.

"We had just arrived in Seoul from Hong Kong when we heard the news," Laura told me forlornly.

"Our vacation, which had been wonderful up to that point, came to a sudden halt. We just didn't know what to do with ourselves," Leigh added. The women then found out that even if they wanted to they couldn't go home.

For hours on end, the sisters were glued to the television in their hotel room. Finally, famished and drained, they ventured out for a quiet meal in one of the restaurants adjacent to the hotel. In the elevator, the sisters quietly discussed their fears. A woman in the elevator bowed her head and said, "I am so sorry for your people." After thanking the woman for her kindness, the twins made their way to the front desk to ask for a restaurant suggestion. The same clerk from the day before was behind the desk and knew the twins were American. "On behalf of all people, I am very sorry," he said through moist eyes. Both Laura and Leigh started to cry. The clerk handed the women tissues, bowed, and made a suggestion for dinner.

As they followed directions to the restaurant, the women noticed a number of people silently walking down one particular street. The group was dressed simply in dark colors; many of the men wore a black armband. Out of curiosity, they followed the throng. As they turned the corner, the sisters found themselves heading toward a local shrine, where people solemnly paid their respects to Americans.

"We held hands and started to cry," Leigh said. "I learned that day that we are really all one people."

> *"Jeong"* is the foundation of Korean culture and permeates all aspects of the culture. Although *jeong* is not translatable to English, it means a combination of empathy, affection, closeness, tenderness, compassion, sentiment, trust, and bonding. *"Mo-jeong"* refers to the relationship between mother and child, *"woo-jeong"* describes the bond between best friends, *"ae-jeong"* expresses the intimacy between lovers, and *"in-jeong"* reflects the universal compassion among all people.

# KALA CHRISTOYENA

ONE OF THE most meaningful Christmas holidays I ever enjoyed was on the Greek island of Crete, and not a single gift was exchanged. The small village I stayed in, located an hour outside of the city of Iraklion, was covered with whitewashed homes. After attending church Christmas morning, the fifty village families that made up the community threw open their doors and welcomed their neighbors with local delicacies and smiles, hugs and exclamations of *"Kala Christouyena,"* or Merry Christmas. As visitors, my family and I were invited to join in the town festivities. As one of our hosts explained to us, in Greece, nobody is a stranger—especially in the outlying villages. Children laughed and played freely in the streets, embraced by mild sunshine. I paraded through the open houses and sampled delicious Greek fare, treating myself to an extra piece of my favorite dessert, baklava, made with walnuts and dripping in honey. Outside we danced in a long line to Greek music, our arms around each other's shoulders and our feet kicking in the air with cries of *"opa."* Christmas took on a new meaning for me that day—a day not to collect "stuff," but to celebrate life and be thankful for family, neighbors, friends, and harmony.

According to a study by economist Joel Waldfogel, much of what we give each other as gifts is a wasted effort. Of the roughly thirty-eight billion dollars that Americans spent on gifts in a recent Christmas season, Walkfogel estimates that between four billion and thirteen billion dollars is spent on gifts that gave no value to the receiver whatsoever.

# CANADIAN CELEBRATIONS

ON AN AUTUMN cruise to Canada, our ship made a stop in Halifax, Nova Scotia. While the sleepy little city boasted few glitzy attractions, the people there had a great deal of civic pride and a strong sense of family. Mandy, our fresh-faced tour guide, greeted us at the bus with a smile.

"Our community and our families are our most intriguing attraction. We have avoided getting caught up in the frenzy that surrounds cities like Toronto and New York," she said. Beaming with pride, she exclaimed that the stores in Halifax are closed on Sundays because "we all need time for our families and friends."

During a brief stop at a beautiful park, I had a few moments to talk to Mandy. "Tell me more about how people here are so connected to their families," I asked her.

"This month, October, is our Thanksgiving," she replied. "However, in my family, we think we should be grateful more than just once a year."

Mandy explained how her family celebrates Thanksgiving quarterly on the last Sunday of every January, April, July, and October. "It's great," she smiled. "All of us get together as a family for a feast and a designated chance to be together." She looked pensive for a moment. "Otherwise, life just gets away from us and we drift. We can't let that happen!"

"Wouldn't it be nice for my family to get together more often," I thought to myself. "Tell me more about your Thanksgivings," I urged. Mandy told me about the standard family menu—braised veal with tomato sauce, tossed salad greens with pecans and blue cheese in an apple vinaigrette, wild rice with mushrooms, and Mandy's personal favorite, brown sugar pie. She gave me the recipe—it's easy to make and you'll love it!

**Brown Sugar Pie**

1 cup brown sugar
1 tablespoon all purpose flour
1 tablespoon butter, softened
4 tablespoon heavy cream
pie crust (use your favorite recipe) with extra dough to create lattice on top

1. Preheat oven to 400° F.
2. In a large mixing bowl, thoroughly combine brown sugar, flour, butter, and cream, then pour into pie crust.
3. Create lattice on top with the extra dough and bake for 30 minutes.
4. Serve to wildly grateful friends and relatives.

The Canadians actually established Thanksgiving forty years prior to the Pilgrims landing in Massachusetts. Canadian Thanksgiving is the second Monday in October, because their harvest season arrives earlier than in the United States.

# LET LIFE IN

WHEN TRACY FOUND herself with ten days off in her flying schedule, she packed a bag and made her way to the airport with no specific destination in mind. (One of the joys of working for an airline is that you can travel virtually anywhere, anytime, for almost nothing.) Gazing up at the flight board, she saw "Bangkok." It sounded exotic, romantic, and fun. Without further ado, she boarded the next flight.

But when she arrived, Tracy discovered a crowded and chaotic metropolis with *tuk-tuks* (motorized bicycles) jockeying for position and zigzagging through a chaotic maze of streets. Smog huddled over the city, making the humidity unbearably suffocating. Angry and disappointed, Tracy began to think seriously about cutting her trip short.

"*Well, I'm here, so I might as well do* something," she grumped to herself. So she lined up for a tour of the Golden Palace, a magnificent, opulent estate that fills a whole city block. Despite herself, she found herself admiring the regal, distinctive splendor of each room as well as the exuberantly ornate architecture of the palace itself. Later, she walked along the water, noticing how the long-tailed boats caressing the canals took on a certain beauty at sunset, and how the majestic temples scattered throughout the ancient city lent it a certain mystery. By evening, she had decided to hold off on any decisions about returning early.

By the third day of her visit, Tracy had ventured beyond "safe" Western–style restaurants and began to sample some of the local specialties. She noticed that on practically every street corner, little eateries featured all manner of delicious-sounding Thai delicacies, including a nearly ubiquitous dish called Green Papaya Salad. She tried this succulent mix of veggies and spices and was immediately hooked. It's easy to make this tempting dish in your own kitchen:

**Green Papaya Salad**

Just mix 2 cups of shredded, not-quite-ripe papaya with one cup of cabbage. Add 3 minced garlic cloves, 3 dried red chilies, $^1/_2$ cup chopped shallots, 3 tablespoons soy sauce, 3 tablespoons lime juice, and peppercorns, cumin, lemongrass, and coriander to taste. Throw in some grilled chicken, fresh tomatoes, and green beans—and you've whipped up a wonderfully healthy and delicious lunch.

For the first time, Tracy felt comfortable dining solo as a single woman. "I struck up conversations with waiters and waitresses, asked them their opinions and chatted with customers at adjoining tables," she told me. "I brought that experience home with me. I no longer hover in my hotel room ordering room service when I am on the road alone. I get out and enjoy the interaction the new environment has to offer."

After a few days, Tracy realized that her body felt lighter and more alive. By the start of week two, she was feeling great! She was eating only fresh, low-calorie yet tasty foods. She was also getting much more exercise than usual, via walking around the bustling city and cycling through the quieter suburbs on a rented bike. Moreover, Tracy found herself striking up dozens of conversations with the gracious, hospitable Thai people, and on several afternoons was invited to tea at the home of a local family. She topped off each day with a hour-long Thai massage, a combination of deep-tissue work and gentle stretching that transformed her into human jelly—for the incredible price of six dollars!

By the time she arrived home—not a minute earlier than originally planned—Tracy was radiant. "I learned a lot about patience," she told me. "And about struggling to stay open and giving opportunities a chance to evolve. If I had stayed stuck in my first impression, I would have been on a plane back to the States the next day!"

*Nothing wrong with home,* I thought to myself. *I love being an American.*

| |
|---|
| There's a whole world out there, waiting to welcome us. |

# SOURCES

At the end of each vignette, I've offered a quote, tip, or fact that I felt was interesting and thought-provoking in light of the story it follows. For some of them, I provided the source as part of the information. The following are my sources for the ones that I chose not to include.

## INTRODUCTION

Mark Olfson, "Changes in the Treatment of Depression in the United States," *Journal of the American Medical Association (JAMA)*, 287, (January 9, 2002), pp. 203–209.

Peter Moore, "The Trouble with Fat Kids," *Men's Health*, October, 2003, p. 100.

American Medical Association (AMA) Web site: www.ama-assn.org.

Divorce Statistics, Divorce Magazine.com: http://www.divorcemag.com/statistics.

Kathleen Deveny, "We're Not in the Mood," *Newsweek Magazine*, June 30, 2003, p. 42.

Ammie N. Feijoo, "Trends in Sexual Risk Among High School Students," Advocates For Youth Home Page: http://www.advocatesforyouth.org/publications/factsheet/fstrends.htm.

Martin Lindstrom, *Brandchild: Remarkable Insights into Today's*

*Global Kids and Their Relationships with Brands,* (London, UK: Kogan Page Business Books, 2003).

## PART 1

Barry Schwartz, *The Paradox of Choice: Why More Is Less* (New York, NY: Ecco Press, 2004).

Listen2Us Web site: http://www.wjoc1490.com. (WJOC online radio, "Wonderful Joy of Christ")

Paul Rozin, Lecture, University of Chicago Alumni Association, Zocalo Restaurant, Philadelphia, PA, November 14, 2002. Paul Rozin is Professor of Psychology at the University of Pennsylvania.

Lee Dye, "Researcher: Giving Can Save Your Life," ABC News, December 12, 2004.

## PART 2

Martin Seligman, *Authentic Happiness: Using the New Positive Psychology to Realize Your Potential for Lasting Fulfillment* (New York, NY: Free Press, 2002).

Maharishi University of Management Web page: www.mum.edu.

Shachi Shantinath, "Take a Deep Breath and Relax," Victim Behavior and Healthy Boundaries Web site, http://victimbehavior.com/breathing/, July 2, 2001.

P. Brown and W. Brown, "Leisure: All Work and No Play Does Jill No Good," *Women's Health Australia: Progress on The Australian Longitudinal Study on Women's Health 1995-2000,* ed. C. Lee (Brisbane, AU: Australian Academic Press, 2001) pp. 153–158.

Jared Sandberg, "Workaholics Use Deception to Check in While on

Vacation," Career Journal.com, The Wall Street Journal Executive Career Site http://www.CareerJournal.com.

Juliet Schor, *The Overspent American* (New York, NY: HarperCollins, 1998), p. 113.

Robert Kriegel, *How to Succeed in Business Without Working So Damn Hard* (New York, NY: Warner Business Books, 2003).

Peter Meiksins and Peter Whalley, *Putting Work in its Place: A Quiet Revolution* (Ithaca, NY: Cornell University Press, 2002).

John Stilgoe, *60 Minutes*, January 4, 2004.

## PART 3

Advocates for Youth Web page: http://www.advocatesforyouth.org.

M.P. Resnick, P. Bearman, and R. Blum, "Protecting Adolescents from Harm," *JAMA (Journal of the American Medical Association)*, 278 (September 10, 1997).

George Mikes, *How to Be an Alien: A Handbook for Beginners and Advanced Pupils*, (London/New York: Wingate, 1946).

Meredith Small, *Our Babies, Ourselves: How Biology and Culture Shape the Way We Parent* (New York, NY: Random House, 1999), see pp. 101, 174, 177–212.

Lorraine Gengo, "Healing Through Touch," *The Fairfield County Weekly*, September 2, 2004, p. 8.

Martin Lindstrom, *Brandchild: Remarkable Insights into the Minds of Today's Global Kids* (London, UK: Kogan Page Business Books, 2003).

New American Dream Web page: www.newamericandream.org.

PART 4

The Official Holland Site—Netherlands Board of Tourism and Conventions (NBTC) Web page: www.holland.com.

Michael Berg, "Biceps Shock: Four New Curls," *Men's Fitness*, July, 2002.

Anne Blair Gould, "Obesity Threatens World's Health," Radio Netherlands homepage, www2.rnw.nl/rnw/en/, July 2002.

Stacy Burling, "The Skinny of Why We're Fat," *The Philadelphia Inquirer,* August 31, 2003.

Ellen Bass, "Childhood Obesity on the Rise," PediatricPlanet.com, http://pediatricplanet.com/.

John Foreyt, "Prevention in Children is Best Option to Combat Obesity Epidemic," keynote lecture at the seventh-annual American College of Sports Medicine Health & Fitness Summit & Exposition, Reno, NV, April 10, 2003.

John P. Robinson, *Time for Life: Surprising Ways Americans Use Their Time* (University Park, PA: The Pennsylvania State University Press, 1999).

PART 5

David Bradley, Home and Garden Web page: http://www.homeandgarden.canoe.ca/.

Paul Wiseman, "No Sex Please—We're Japanese." USA Today, June 3, 2004, p. 17A.

*Divorce* magazine Web site: www.divorcemag.com/statistics/statsworld/shtml.

Noelle Knox, "European Gay-Union Trends Influence U.S. Debate," *USA Today,* July 13, 2004.

## PART 6

Kathleen Deveny, "We're Not in The Mood, " *Newsweek Magazine,* June 30, 2003, pp. 42–43.

Lisa Frydman, "Women Far More Forgiving About Sex and Weight," *Chicago Sun Times,* September 17, 2004.

"Sex in America 50 years after the Kinsey Report," *HealthState, The Magazine of the University of Medicine and Dentistry of New Jersey,* Spring/Summer 1999, http://www.umdnj.edu/umcweb/marketing_and_communications/publications/umdnj_magazine/hstate/sum99/sex_kinsey.htm.

Esther Perel, "Erotic Intelligence," *Psychotherapy Networker,* May/June 2003, pp. 25–53.

Sergio Luis de Freitas, *International Encyclopedia of Sexuality,* (New York, NY: Continuum International Publishing Group, 2004).

Robert Tagadora, "French Public Opinion on Important Issues of the Day." *Priorities and Frivolities,* November 6, 2003.

Laura Berman, Network for Excellence in Women's Sexual Health Web page: http://www.newshe.com/articles.

Feijoo, Ammie N. "Adolescent Sexual Health in Europe and the U.S. — Why the Difference?" Advocates for Youth Web page: www.advocatesforyouth.org/publications/factsheet/fsest.pdf. October, 2001.

## PART 7

Annetta Miller, *Sharing Boundaries: Learning the Wisdom of Africa* (Nairobi: Paulines Publications Africa, 2003), p. 48.

Mary Sanchez, "Cheers for Mexico's Concept of Death," *San Diego Union Tribune,* October 30, 2004.

Belief Net Web site: www.belief.net.

## PART 8

Law School Admission Council Web page: www.lsac.org.

Alcoholics Anonymous Web Page, www.alcoholics-anonymous.org.

P.A. Glare, B. Tobin, C. J. Ryan, and M. Kaye. "Euthanasia in Australia—The Northern Territory of the Terminally Ill Act." *New England Journal of Medicine,* 334, (February 1, 1996).

Indigenous Peoples Literature Web page: www.indigenouspeople.net.

National Center for Educational Statistics Web page: www.nces.ed.gov.

Sheldon Kramer, "Jewish Spiritual Pathways for Growth and Healing," in *Modern Psychology and Ancient Wisdom,* edited by Sharon G. Mijares (Binghamptom, NY: Haworth Press, 2003) p. 100.

Niall Ferguson, "The End of Europe?" *American Enterprise Institute for Public Policy Research Newsletter,* April 2004.

## PART 9

Random Acts of Kindness Foundation Web page, Health Benefits Section. "Kindness: How Good Deeds Can Be Good For You." www.actsofkindness.org/inspiration/health/index.asp.

Helen Exley. *Smile.* Helen Exley Giftbooks, www.helenexleygiftbooks.com.

Meredith F. Small, *Our Babies, Ourselves: How Biology and Culture Shape the Way We Parent* (New York, NY: Anchor, 1999), p. 120.

Miller, *Sharing Boundaries,* pp. 10, 18.

Schor, *The Over Spent American,* p. 89.

# ACKNOWLEDGMENTS

TO MY FORMER coworkers at People Express and USAirways, who endured uncertain and turbulent times in the airline industry with dignity and grace, my fond memories and compassion.

To my peers at JetBlue Airways, who contribute to such a marvelous and upbeat culture, my loyalty and commitment.

To Chris Collins, who believed in my talents and created a wonderful career opportunity, my admiration and friendship.

To Bill O'Hanlon, who provided the writing workshop and foundation for this book, my gratitude.

To my editor, Marian Sandmaier, whose guidance and wisdom kept me focused, my respect.

To my agent, Linda Konner, whose direction and counsel I rely on, my trust.

To my publisher, Sue McCloskey, who took a chance on a new writer, my thanks.